KU-350-592

HAMPSHIRE
and the
ISLE OF WIGHT

A. Temple Patterson

HAMPSHIRE
and the
ISLE OF WIGHT

B. T. Batsford Ltd,
London

First published 1976

© A. Temple Patterson 1976

Typeset by
Input Typesetting Ltd, London
and printed by The Pitman Press Ltd
Bath
for the publishers, B. T. Batsford Ltd
4 Fitzhardinge Street, London W1H 0AH

ISBN 0 7134 3221 7

Contents

Illustrations

Acknowledgments

The Author and Publishers would like to thank the following for permission to reproduce the photographs in this book: Peter Baker Photography Ltd no. 23; J. Allan Cash Ltd nos. 3, 5, 15, 20, 25; A. F. Kersting, F.R.P.S. nos. 2, 7, 8, 9, 10, 11, 12, 16, 17, 19, 22, 24; Kenneth Scowen, FII.P., F.R.P.S., nos. 4, 6, 13, 18; Olive Smith (the late Edwin Smith) nos. 1, 14; Spectrum Colour Library no. 21.

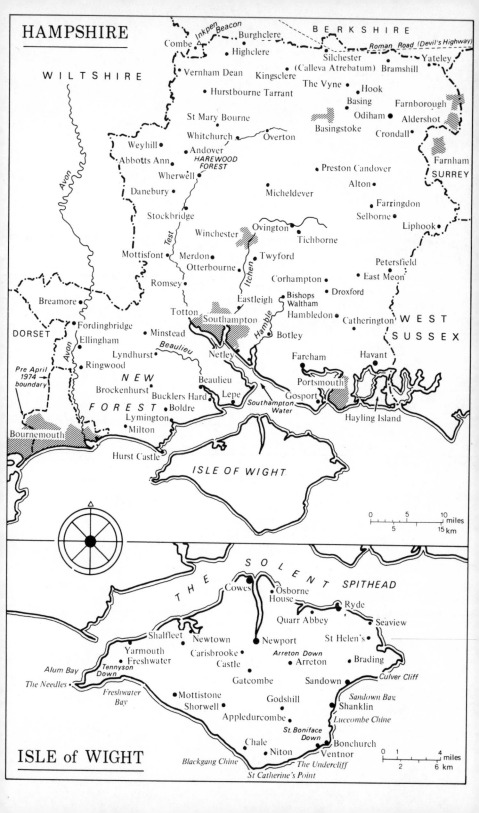

Introduction

Hampshire probably conjures up for those who know something of it one or other of two widely different pictures, or perhaps both. One is that which shows itself to those who come to it by road or rail from London or the Thames valley; though it stands out more clearly if they come by road, and best of all if they have leisure to turn aside from its trunk arteries and linger in its little towns and villages and its still comparatively tranquil countryside. This is a picture of a county that remains largely rural, with some of the finest scenery in the south of England; ranging from the pinewoods and sandy heaths that border Surrey, through the neighbouring clay country in the north-east with its villages and valleys, streams and small fields; and then the rolling chalk downlands of the centre and north-west that form the water-parting between the Thames and Hampshire Basins, where the nucleated villages cling close to the scarpfoot springs because of the problem of water supply. Here are the wide sweeping downs that are perhaps the county's most characteristic feature together with its forest and river country. South of them the clay rises uppermost again and the villages are straggling and rather shapeless. Then come the heaths and commons and the majestic oaks and conifers of the New Forest; while in the Isle of Wight the chalk downs reappear. Along the western border of the shire, too, runs that narrow rim of upper greensand which has given rise to the cliff-like wooded hangers that are almost peculiar to the Hampshire landscape.

In one way it can be said that this is the face of Hampshire which tends to emerge from its earlier history, for the majority of the Saxons who settled in it after the end of Roman rule in this island are now

thought by several historians to have made their way southwards from the
middle Thames; though the ruling house and its immediate followers —
not to mention a rather mysterious Jutish element — came inland from
landings on its south coast.

Nevertheless Hampshire is *Hampton*shire, 'Hamtunscir' as the
Anglo-Saxon Chronicle calls it. It takes its name, that is, from the town
that for long was often called just 'Hampton' and was the ancestor or
nucleus of the modern Southampton. And so the other picture of the
county is that which presents itself to those who come to it or leave it by
sea. This is also a picture which reflects its early — indeed its very early —
history. Its deeply indented coast has given it two great natural harbours
that are approached through waters sheltered by the Isle of Wight and are
nowadays maintained by persistent dredging to meet the needs of modern
ships. Opposite this coast the Cotentin peninsula projects from the
Continent, ensuring in early days a crossing which was in sight of land for
much of the way and whose importance as early as the Bronze Age is
proved by finds made by archaeologists. In these and even earlier times
the twin rivers Test and Itchen that drain both the county's chalk plateau
and the sands and clays of the broad shallow valley to the south of it,
gave a relatively easy access to the interior such as no other inlets along
the whole of our south coast could offer. Archaeology suggests that when
about 2500 B.C. the technique of agriculture first spread to Britain, these
two rivers must have given the primitive farming peoples of the Neolithic
or New Stone Age passages through the forest to the downlands beyond.
It also shows quite definitely that during the later part of the Bronze Age
which began a few hundred years afterwards traders travelled to and fro
along these waterways exchanging new tools for old and broken ones;
indeed several buried hoards of their stock-in-trade have been found in
this neighbourhood, perhaps hastily hidden in some emergency and never
afterwards retrieved. And the Itchen in particular, whose upper course is
separated only by a low watershed from that of the river Wey and so
from the Thames Basin, presently provided a highway to the latter and
thus to London when it came into existence. Hence Hampshire has for
long been a gateway, one of the three main entrances to southern England
from the Continent, the others being London and Plymouth.

It is therefore a county with two aspects, coastal and hinterland, and in
order to see it as a whole one must understand and linger over them both,

appreciating the history, interest and attractions of its great ports not less than those of its countryside. But from which direction is it best to begin one's approach? A drawback to looking at it first with the eye of a traveller coming from London is that the two main roads into it from this direction enter by way of Basingstoke and Aldershot respectively, and neither is typical of Hampshire. Basingstoke, which not so very long ago was a sleepy country town, dismissed almost contemptuously by some previous writers on the county as a colourless place with few or no attractions, has recently undergone a remarkable transformation through the planned overspill of industry and population from Greater London. Already quadrupled or quintupled in size and still growing fast, it has become an up-and-coming industrial town of quite considerable importance, which is interesting as an economic phenomenon and an example of our newest industrial revolution. But it is not specifically Hampshire; the London overspill has taken other directions also and similar phenomena have occurred or are occurring elsewhere. And though Aldershot's importance as a major military centre is obvious and there is at least one other military area in the county, it also is not typical. Moreover though it has been improved architecturally of late it has not been a pretty town, and indeed it is not very long since it was acidly described as a large and hideous conglomeration of buildings looking as though they might be packed up and removed at a moment's notice by a fatigue squad.

There is however a third possibility. Since Winchester is the county town and was once the capital of the Saxon kingdom of Wessex and indeed for several centuries that of England (though to call it a capital rather than use some such phrase as 'the king's chief residence' is to risk giving too modern an impression), and since nine roads radiate from it, might it not be best to start from there and work outwards, as has been admirably done before? Moreover, Winchester lies within the chalk downlands whose sweeping vistas are so characteristic of the county, and on one of its best-known rivers. Once more it might be argued that history endorses such an approach; for it is in the gravel terraces of some of these rivers that there have been found the hand axes and other primitive tools of palaeolithic men which are the earliest evidences of human settlement; and it was on the downs that their Neolithic successors, who were the first to leave any visible field monuments, built their long barrows or mounds covering collective burials. On the downs again the thousand and more round barrows of the Bronze Age men who came after them were mainly concentrated; and it is on the downs once more that the small embanked 'Celtic' fields of this latter period may be traced; while the subsequent Iron Age crowned them with hill forts such as Quarley, Danebury and the unfinished stronghold on Ladle Hill.

Winchester, too, can claim to be the oldest town in the county, though by a rather narrow margin over Southampton; for before the Romans came there had been a settlement there of Belgae, a people of mixed Gaulish and Germanic stock of whom some offshoots had established themselves in south-east Britain in the last century B.C. This settlement became the Romano-British town of Venta Belgarum – Venta of the Belgae. The rest of the region that was afterwards to be Hampshire remained essentially agricultural under the Romans, farmed by a scattered population living in buildings that varied from peasant huts to the 70 or more villas now known to have existed in the county. The only other town, apart from Venta's port of Clausentum near the mouth of the Itchen which may be called the first Southampton, was Calleva Atrebatum (Silchester) on the northern fringe of the area, with a hinterland that was more outside it than within; and its site had afterwards so little attraction for Saxon and Norman settlers that unlike Winchester it has remained virtually uninhabited since the Roman period ended in the fifth century.

Nevertheless nearly 70 years ago D. H. Moutray Reid wrote in his *Highways and Byways of Hampshire*: 'How more fittingly can we enter the county than through Southampton?', and perhaps it may be an acceptable compromise to do that first and then move on to Winchester and proceed from there.

Partly (but only partly) because of its close connection with the fighting services through Portsmouth, Hampshire can boast, if it needed to boast, of such a galaxy of great names as few other counties can show; from the Roman admiral Carausius who probably built the fortress at Portchester to the Southampton-born Earl Jellicoe who commanded the Grand Fleet in the First World War. There is the Saxon monk Winfrith, admittedly a Devonian by birth, who went out from Nursling to meet a martyr's death while converting Germany to Christianity and is better known as St Boniface; Alfred the Great, whose bones lie at Winchester

1   Opposite *The south work of the nave of Winchester cathedral as reconstructed in the fourteenth century: the most splendid transformation in the cathedral's history.*

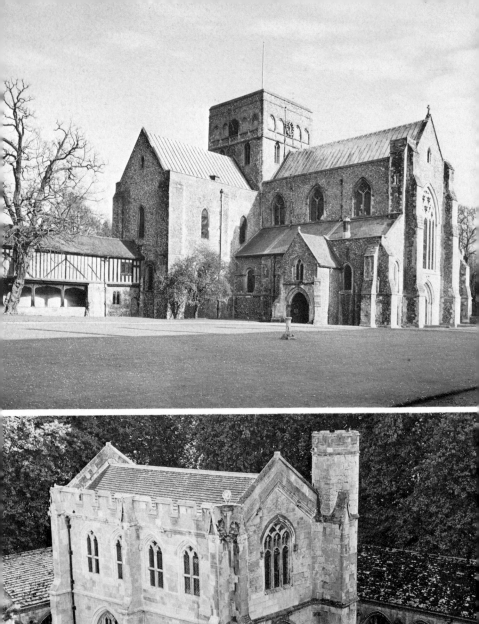

and whose statue dominates its High Street; William of Wykeham, the master builder who not only rebuilt the nave of its cathedral and founded Winchester College but gave England such grand memorials as his work in Windsor Castle and New College, Oxford; William Lily, the pioneer of the Renaissance who first taught Greek in England; the Paulet Marquesses of Winchester, the first Marquess who was minister to four Tudor sovereigns and of whom Queen Elizabeth I said that if only he were a young man she would rather have him as a husband than any other man in England, and the fifth Marquess who in the Civil War held Basing House against the Parliamentarians for three years until it was stormed by Cromwell himself; Gibbon and Gilbert White; the Portals and the Barings, immigrants of the seventeenth and eighteenth centuries respectively whose families have played great parts in English history as manufacturers and merchants, statesmen and empire-builders, soldiers and airmen; Anson and Hawke, Rodney, Hood and Nelson; Wellington in his years of retirement and repose; Jane Austen and Mary Mitford; William Cobbett and John Keble; Florence Nightingale and Lord Palmerston; Dickens and Meredith, Kingsley and Tennyson.

It has been said that Hampshire is not a county of great architecture, either ecclesiastical (apart from Winchester Cathedral, Romsey Abbey and East Meon parish church) or domestic. This is perhaps an over-sweeping statement. It is true that it lies entirely outside the ribbon of England's best building stone, the oolitic limestone which two of its neighbours, Dorset and Wiltshire, share; though it has some good limestone in the Isle of Wight and there is plenty of flint and chalk (or malm) and of course brick. Nevertheless, to make a cursory survey beginning with the Saxon period, the recent excavations of Winchester Cathedral's tenth-century predecessor and of the Saxon church at Breamore would by themselves put the county on any map of Anglo-Saxon buildings, and in Saxon stone sculpture it is supreme, as witness the famous Romsey Rood. For the Norman period it has four of the country's ten Tournai marble fonts and many churches besides the three cited above that have major Norman elements, such as Pamber Priory, St Michael's at Southampton, Portchester and Petersfield (the last two of which are virtually entirely Norman). The flower of its achievement in church architecture, however, blossomed during the transition from the Norman to the Early English style in the period c.

2   Opposite above *The church of St Cross Hospital near Winchester: one of the finest specimens of transitional Norman architecture in England.*

3   Opposite below *The chantry of Winchester College.*

1180 – c. 1220. The Decorated style is poorly represented, but it is rich in Perpendicular, though, on the whole, not in the parish churches. It was not much of a castle county, but it has three major monuments in the keep and curtain wall of Portchester and the ruins of the two palaces of the bishops of Winchester at Wolvesey and Bishops Waltham; as well as Odiham Castle with the only octagonal keep in England. The medieval walls of Southampton with their magnificent Bargate are among the two or three finest in the country and to them must be added the remains of Norman and thirteenth-century merchants' houses there, of which more have been revealed by recent excavation. In Winchester Castle Hall, moreover, Hampshire has the finest medieval hall in England next to Westminster's.

One great lack that must be admitted, however, is that in a county so poor in building stone strangely little use was made of timber, for there are no really interesting timber-framed houses, apart perhaps from the Tudor House at Southampton.

There are also only three country houses of major architectural importance regularly open to the public now that Bramshill has become a police college and is not available: namely, The Vyne, Mottisfont and Breamore. Nevertheless there are many interesting smaller ones such as Avington, Stratfield Saye and Grove Place near Southampton. These are often surrounded by good gardens and are accessible to visitors on certain days during the summer, and there are others, especially in the Isle of Wight, whose exterior attractiveness at least can be seen; while some of the small towns that are far enough away from London's overspill to be untouched by it have outstanding charm and even beauty. Modern architecture is seen at its best in the Wessex Hotel at Winchester and perhaps at Southampton, while some good examples have made or are making their appearance at Portsmouth and Basingstoke.

It is significant that nearly all of Hampshire's few outstanding country houses lie near its boundaries and away from the central chalk country: Bramshill, The Vyne, Stratfield Saye and Hackwood in the north; Mottisfont and Breamore in the west; and Grove Place in the south. The exceptions are The Grange near Alresford, and Avington; and the former blossomed from a middle-sized house into a fine mansion on the strength of money which came from banking and not from the land, while the latter lies in a river valley. Similarly, the comparatively few fine churches in the county – with some rare exceptions such as East Meon – are to be found away from the chalk subsoil. Most Hampshire churches, in the country areas at least, have more antiquity than magnitude, and there are not many to compare with those of Norfolk or Gloucestershire. What this location of the great houses and modest size of the churches in the central districts betokens is that in past centuries the chalk and clay areas were not good arable land though somewhat better for sheep-pasture. However modern methods have changed all this, and they now vie with the best corn-growing regions in England.

Hampshire farming to-day falls into two categories, broadly speaking: this chalkland farming, mainly of barley though with a secondary activity; and the smaller and more varied kinds away from the chalk. There has also been a general trend towards larger farming units in the county as a whole. Wheat, which reached a high acreage during the war years of 1939-45, decreased again afterwards in view of barley's greater profitability. Oats also declined, though more because mechanisation was replacing horses in farmwork. The increased size of farms has shown itself particularly in dairy-farming, though since 1950 there are fewer farmers keeping herds of dairy cows, and also in pig-rearing and poultry-farming; while the long decline in the number of sheep has latterly been arrested. These trends towards monoculture on the chalk, larger units in general, and dairying and poultry-farming on a large scale have been made possible by increased use of modern fertilisers, improvements in mechanisation, farm buildings, transport and marketing, and by the consequent economical use of a dwindling labour force. In some areas machinery syndicates serve the needs of groups of farmers, while there are also building syndicates for grain drying and storage. The larger and more profitable farms are mostly on the chalk, which may be taken as stretching down to a line a mile or so north of Eastleigh and Portsmouth; though some are to be found in smaller areas outside the chalk belt: the Martin-Rockbourne salient that protrudes into Dorset, the northern slopes of Portsdown Hill, and some of the intensive areas between Southampton and Fareham and between the Solent and the New Forest. The small and medium-sized farms, some of them below the national productivity average, lie in and around the Test valley between the chalk and the New Forest (which is mainly non-agricultural Crown land), as well as in the Avon valley, that part of the London Basin which stretches down into north-east Hampshire, and the urban ribbon extension north of Portsmouth.

Books about Hampshire and descriptions of it in the writings of travellers and the like are legion, and selection is invidious, but perhaps it may be attempted. In the sixteenth century the traveller John Leland saw it as a county with a comparatively small rural population and a few towns whose prosperity showed itself in the new Tudor houses of which the Manor of God-Begot in Winchester High Street and what is to-day called the Tudor House at Southampton are survivals. More than a century and a half later another intrepid and persistent traveller, Celia Fiennes, who knew Hampshire well and often visited her relations there, recorded her impressions in her journal, apparently in 1702. She visited the great mansions and many of the lesser country houses, at some of which latter she stayed; but she was also interested in local industries such as the salt-panning works at Lymington where she described in detail – she had a great eye for detail – the apparatus used. Southampton she found a declining but clean town, and at Portsmouth she inspected the fortifications and went on board two of the Navy's largest warships. Daniel Defoe, whose *Tour through the Whole Island of Great Britain* was published in 1724, included accounts of the visits he paid, being a townsman with an appreciation of trade, to Hampshire towns. He also recorded the importance of Lymington's salt-making industry and found Southampton rather decayed but Portsmouth prosperous. Winchester he reported as having no trade or manufacture, but full of social life, not least among its numerous and well-to-do clergy.

Unlike Defoe, William Cobbett was essentially a countryman, who farmed in Hampshire for thirteen years (1804-17) and whose *Rural Rides* afterwards often took him to or through the county. In 1821, the first of the years which he recorded, he rode no fewer than six times over the hills of north-west Hampshire, avoiding (as was his wont) the turnpike roads whenever he could, the better to look at the crops of the landowners and farmers by whose estates and farms he passed. His favourite halting-place was the house of a farmer friend in the village of Hurstbourne Tarrant, though he also liked to visit William Chamberlayne at Weston near Southampton, a landowner to whom he gave the highest praise for his generosity to his labourers and his general benevolence. This was a period of agricultural depression, however, and Cobbett was much more often lamenting the gradual disappearance of the smallholders and denouncing the low wages paid to farmworkers and the savage punishment of the poaching to which some of them were driven by sheer necessity. As a leading Radical journalist and publicist he also took every opportunity of addressing meetings in the country towns through which he passed. His friend Squire Chamberlayne, it should be explained, was not only a liberal and progressive landowner but also an independent Whig member of Parliament for Southampton and therefore at least able to tolerate his views.

One of the best-known of the agricultural riots leading to attacks on workhouses which broke out in this period of distress, that at Selborne in 1830, was well described by the naturalist W. H. Hudson in *Hampshire Days*, which is among the most delightful books ever written about the county. Born in 1841 in South America, where as a boy he ran wild on the farms and ranches of the Rio de la Plata and watched the bird-life of the great plains, he came to England at the age of 28 and at first lived in considerable poverty amid drab London boarding-house surroundings. His first books had no great sale, but his *The Naturalist in La Plata* brought him into prominence and afterwards they commanded an increasing circulation. Possessing an absolute freedom of spirit together with great sensitiveness and receptivity and an almost mystical sense of natural beauty, he expounded in them a philosophy of life based on observation of the animal world. In *Afoot in England*, a predecessor of *Hampshire Days*, he described the Hampshire highlands and the Bourne valley, where he had visited the house in which Cobbett had stayed at Hurstbourne Tarrant. In the closing years of the nineteenth century he wandered all over the county, and in 1900 he stayed alone for a summer in (the then) Sir Edward Grey's fishing cottage (he called Grey a Northumbrian with Hampshire written in his heart) in the Itchen valley.

Histories of Hampshire have been written by the Rev. Richard Warner, curate to the naturalist William Gilpin at Boldre in the New Forest (in outline in 1792), Robert Mudie (in three volumes in 1838-40), the Rev. Woodward (also in three volumes, undated) and T. W. Shore in 1892, among others. Shore was for 23 years secretary of the Hartley Institution in Southampton which developed into first the University College in 1902 and then the University in 1952. At the Institution he laid the foundation of what is now a fine collection of books on local history and of prints; and he was also a founder member of the Hampshire Field Club and Archaeological Society, which still flourishes.

In the wake of these early travellers and historians came many authors of histories of particular towns and regions of the county and of topographical works, rather. too numerous for individual mention here and now sometimes or somewhat outdated by the far-reaching changes which are taking place in southern Hampshire and in the Basingstoke and Andover areas, but which nevertheless provide pictures of the Hampshire which preceded these modern developments and still partly survives.

ONE

Southampton

The traveller by sea enters the port of Southampton as soon as his ship begins to move up that great estuary of its twin rivers which is called Southampton Water, though he does not reach the city itself till shortly below their confluence, since it is on the peninsula they form as they come together that what is still the greater part of it stands. Meanwhile the seven-mile journey up to the docks whose starting-point projects from that peninsula is full of interest. The eastern side of the estuary, with its low wooded shores sloping to a muddy marge, is not much industrialized, though oil-storage depots have spread across from the vast Fawley refinery on the other side to compete for prominence with the yachts at Hamble where the tributary river of that name comes in. Only after the tower of Netley Castle and the brand-new skyscraper blocks of flats that dwarf it at Weston Shore have been passed do the shipyards begin at Woolston. This suburb of Southampton, lying downwater across the Itchen from the bulk of the city, was once hailed by over-optimistic citizens as its budding Birkenhead; but this it has never become, though the parent port overhauled Liverpool in passenger traffic at least, as well as becoming a leading cargo emporium.

The western shore of Southampton Water is more industrialized. Just inside it, Calshot Castle on its projecting spit of land – one of the coastal forts built by Henry VIII to protect the country against French attacks – is overshadowed by an electricity generating station. Northward comes the huge Esso oil refinery at Fawley, which was once the sleepiest village in Hampshire, mocked in the seventeenth century for having allegedly known nothing about the Civil War until it was over. This refinery, which has contributed notably to Southampton's prosperity, was opened in 1951 and is the largest in Britain and the second largest in Europe. Its annual capacity of 19 million tons of crude oil represents over 15% of the country's refining capacity, and a significant proportion of its products are exported. Nearly 4000 vessels a year and more than 18 million gallons a day of crude oil or refined products are handled at its Marine Terminal; while the refinery and its associated industrial plants cover some 1700 acres of former heathland. Northward again along the western shore is Hythe, swelling rapidly as the result of a planned post-war expansion into a little town associated with the Fawley industries, but with a disjointed and rather distressing series of private housing estates as its hinterland. Next comes the Marchwood power-station, which some have considered one of the best pieces of post-war industrial architecture in Britain while others hold that it sticks out like a sore thumb against the background of New Forest woodlands. Fawley, it may be added, has an even bigger power-station, but since it is built partly underground it is less prominent.

Of the three main landward approaches to Southampton the most attractive is that from the north by the road from Winchester, notwithstanding the enormous and almost frightening roundabout to which the traveller comes soon after passing the city boundary. Here the journey onward from the well-to-do suburb of Bassett down the tree-lined Avenue across the Common – a remarkable open space to find within the confines of a large town – is as pleasant and even striking as modern traffic conditions will allow; indeed it must be among the most impressive entrances to any city in the kingdom. The approach from the east has one outstanding moment when after crossing the Hamble at the yachting village of Bursledon and passing through large areas of Corporation housing the road comes suddenly to the brow of Lance's Hill, from which those who are safely on the pavement can survey the main bulk of the city spread out below them with the Itchen in the foreground and a surprising amount of woodland interspersed among the suburbs to the right. The entry from the west is perhaps the dullest once the New Forest has been left behind; though after crossing the Test just above where it broadens out abruptly into Southampton Water and by-passing the village of Redbridge, whose High Street has some pleasant Georgian and earlier brick houses, the road into the heart of the city runs alongside the estuary, past the New Docks and the light industries of the Millbrook Estate.

Essentially and by origin, Southampton is a confluence town which grew up on the kind of site likely to be chosen early for occupation, since besides being protected on two sides by rivers and originally also by their marshes and muddy foreshores it could offer occasional 'hards' – patches of dry and firm ground or of gravel, created by currents or eddies and sloping up from these foreshores to provide safe landing-places. Moreover it had a further great advantage in that here there occurred a very rare phenomenon, a confluence of rivers close to a seafront, producing a port well served by tides and yet far enough inland to be reasonably sheltered – 'a seaport without the sea's terrors, an ocean approach within the threshold of the land', as it has been put. This approach was sheltered further by the Isle of Wight, which in addition gave Southampton a double high-tide by providing two entrances to the Solent, with the result that the ebb after the up-Channel tide through the western one is checked by a second and later high-tide through the eastern entrance. For eight and a quarter hours the water-level at Southampton is either rising or standing, while the ebb lasts only three and three quarters. This prolonged period of relatively high water made it easy for the ships of early centuries to unload their cargoes.

Nevertheless the first Southampton, apart from a few traces of prehistoric settlement, was not on the peninsula between the Test and Itchen at all, but on the much smaller Bitterne peninsula, jutting out from the east bank of the Itchen a mile or more as the crow flies above its junction with the Test and about three miles from that as the river winds. This was the Romano-British port of Clausentum, which came into existence in the later part of the first century A.D., very soon after the coming of the Romans. Here were landed those products of Roman industry on the Continent for which the romanized local aristocracy who lived in Venta or in country villas had developed a taste: great jars of wine and oil and red-glazed Samian ware from Gaul, such as can be seen to-day in Southampton's God's House Museum. In exchange, corn, wool, oysters, slaves and lead were shipped across the Channel. Clausentum seems to have been abandoned soon after the close of the Roman period and its site is now enclosed within the grounds of Bitterne Manor on the far side of Northam Bridge, though the last traces of its buildings disappeared only late in the nineteenth century.

By the eighth century, however, a trading settlement called Hamwi or Hamwic had been established lower down the river on its opposite or western bank (more or less round the site of the modern St Mary's church) and had taken over the function of a port to Winchester which Clausentum had exercised in Roman times. Whether this was the 'Hamtun' which afterwards gave its name to the shire, or whether as has been suggested Hamtun was a separate settlement on the higher ground west of Hamwic and close to the Test estuary (about where Portland Street is now), remains controversial; but so far there has not been much archaeological evidence in support of the latter theory, and it was the last mouldering ruins of Hamwic that were known as 'Old Hampton' in the fifteenth century.

Like Clausentum before it Hamwic imported chiefly luxuries and exported mainly woollen cloth and slaves. Excavation has brought to light fragments of pottery jars and flagons that had contained wine, decanters and cups of fine coloured glass, and blocks of lava used for making millstones; all of them articles which had been produced in the Rhineland and northern France, though the trading contacts of the port seem to have extended to the Baltic and even the Mediterranean. But from the ninth century onwards Hamwic suffered from Viking raids and presently its harbour began to silt up. By the time of the Norman Conquest it had shrunk to a few houses and a church.

Even before the Conquest, however, a town which came to be known as 'Suthhamtun' or South Hampton was developing on the southern part of the peninsula between the Test and the Itchen, and it benefited considerably from the change of rulers in 1066. Since it was the natural port of transit between Normandy and Winchester, and the latter remained for some time longer what may be loosely called the capital of England, the modest trade which it and Hamwic before it had enjoyed in Saxon times was much increased. Moreover, its position in the centre of the south coast and its relationship to a wide and accessible hinterland gave it advantages as a distributing and collecting centre for the commerce of a considerable area which some of the Norman merchants who had followed the Conqueror were quick to appreciate. Although till recently the loss of Normandy by King John was thought to have dealt a severe blow to its trade, the excavations conducted in parts of the old town by Dr Colin Platt of Southampton University and his colleagues have shown that full and even more than full compensation was found in the growth of the trade in wine from Gascony, much of which had remained linked to England, as well as by participation in the expanding wool-trade with Flanders. By 1300 Southampton had become one of the leading ports of the country.

After the Conquest the central thoroughfare of the town, running north and south (the later High Street), had become known as English Street, while the two parallel streets to the west of it, made somewhat shorter by the building of a castle in the north-west corner of the town, were named or renamed French Street and Bull Street respectively and constituted the French quarter. Within this, the Norman and other French merchants established themselves along the as yet unwalled western shore to the south of the castle. Here they built fine stone houses with quays and wharfage of their own which had easy access to the sea. The remains of one such house, which has been called one of the finest examples of Norman domestic architecture surviving in England, have long been open to view from the garden of what is now the Tudor House Museum; and Dr Platt's excavations have uncovered others to the south of it. Evidently, however, the successful merchants began presently to move round into the lower part of English Street, for the remains of another large two-storeyed house, dating from the late twelfth century and miscalled 'Canute's Palace' through the romantic imagination of an early nineteenth-century antiquarian, have survived in Porters Lane which leads into the High Street from the foot of French Street; while the bombing in the Second World War laid bare many late twelfth- and thirteenth-century vaults in this area which can still be seen and had originally been constructed under houses of that period for the storage of wine and other merchandise. Substantial houses of this sort soon stretched along the whole lower length of English Street.

The layout of the old town was thus on a grid pattern, with English Street as its central axis and feeder lanes running off it to either side, but mostly to French Street on the west. This pattern remained almost unchanged until in recent years the drastic demands of modern traffic brought into being a ring road that smashed through the north walls, absorbed the greater part of French Street and swept eastwards across the lower High Street. Bugle Street, as Bull Street had been renamed in the later eighteenth century ('bugle' being an obsolete or dialect word for a young bull) was left for a time more of a quiet backwater than ever until still more recently an early twentieth-century municipal housing scheme which formed its upper part was demolished. On the other side of English Street there were fewer lanes, but from it East Street led to the now vanished East Gate and then crossed the town ditch or moat that lay outside the eastern and northern walls to continue as a kind of medieval ribbon development lined with houses and small shops as far as St Mary's church, the twelfth-century successor to Hamwic's Saxon minster. This twelfth-century church was itself pulled down in the 1540s during a war with France because, it is said, the townsfolk feared that its splendid spire towering up to the east of the town might guide the French to it. It was not fully replaced until 1711, when a third church was built which in its turn gave place to yet another St Mary's in the 1870s. North of the town another ribbon development extended beyond the magnificent North or Bar Gate, which was constructed in stages between the twelfth and fifteenth centuries.

Although Southampton lived primarily by seaborne trade and its life was therefore dominated by its merchants and shipowners, it was no more divorced from the land and the life of the land than any other medieval English town. Many of the burgesses still combined their buying and selling or even their overseas ventures with the cultivation of the surrounding fields and the tending of their cattle. In fact it is unique among English towns in having kept almost intact the original common lands that once provided its main food-supply and merely transformed them into public parks and city 'lungs'. They include both what were once the common arable fields in which individual townsmen held strips of land – Houndwell, Hoglands and the East and West Marlands – and the common pastures, including the present Common which was acquired from what was then the neighbouring manor of Shirley in 1228. 'Marlands', incidentally, is a corruption of Magdalens, a name derived from a leper hospital dedicated to St Mary Magdalen which was established in these fields about the twelfth century at what was then a safe distance from the town.

In the later Middle Ages Southampton developed a trade with the commercial republics of Venice and Genoa which made it the chief centre of Italian commerce with England. Italian business firms established

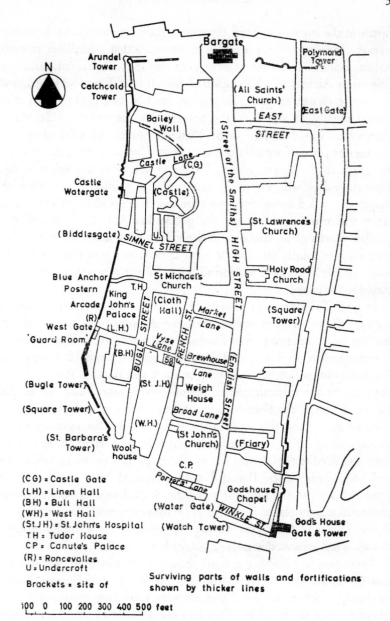

Detailed Plan of medieval walled town of Southampton, from Collected Essays on Southampton, *published on behalf of Southampton (then) County Borough Council.*

agents in the town who lived there with their families, clerks, household
servants and sometimes even African slaves, so that a small but vigorous
Italian colony grew up. Some even became naturalised, and one
Cristoforo Ambruogi who anglicised his name as Christopher Ambrose
was twice chosen mayor. The visiting carracks and galleys often spent
several months at a time in the port; and a chapel behind St Mary's
church that was dedicated to St Nicholas, the patron saint of seamen,
became the place of worship of their crews. Here a mural tablet recorded
the burial in a common grave of some of the Slavonian oarsmen of a
Venetian galley who had happened to die at Southampton. When the
chapel was pulled down along with the church in the sixteenth century the
tablet was transferred (though the galleys had just ceased to come) to
another church of St Nicholas in the village of North Stoneham, which
even now is a little outside the city. In modern times this has puzzled
many people who have wondered why the oarsmen should have been
buried so far inland.

In later Tudor days Southampton declined. The fundamental reasons
for the collapse of its prosperity were the growth of London's trade and
the resultant tendency for English commerce and shipping to be
concentrated in the Thames. Hitherto the relatively easy land route from
Southampton to London, mainly over chalk and Bagshot sand, had been
preferred to the difficult and dangerous sea voyage round the Kentish
Forelands and up the Thames. But now improvements in shipbuilding and
pilotage had made this easier than before; while the opening by the
Portuguese of the Cape route to the East had transferred the spice trade
from the Mediterranean and the hands of the Italians to Lisbon at first
and afterwards, when Portugal was conquered for a period by the
Spaniards who at that time also ruled the Netherlands, to Antwerp which
was conveniently placed for London. In the seventeenth century the town
shrank into a regional port serving the needs of the Hampshire Basin,
though it still imported wine for a somewhat wider area.

There was one striking episode, however. It was from Southampton
that in 1620 the Puritans who are known as the Pilgrim Fathers
originally sailed in two small and not very seaworthy vessels named the
Mayflower and the *Speedwell*. They had not intended to put in at any other
English port, but on their way down-Channel the ill-named *Speedwell*
proved so leaky that she had to be abandoned at Plymouth and the whole

company re-embarked there in the *Mayflower*. That they had left Southampton believing that they would never again set foot on English ground is therefore not widely known outside the town except by those who have seen the tall Pilgrim Fathers Memorial that was erected in 1913 on the Western Esplanade not far from the now-vanished West Quay from which they sailed.

In the eighteenth century Southampton found a new prosperity and even fame with the discovery of mineral springs to the north of the old walls at a spot still marked by the secluded Spa Tavern near Portland Street. Bathing, for which a vogue was beginning, also developed in spite of the fact that the town had no sandy beach but only a muddy foreshore, a defect that was remedied by various enterprising individuals who established baths near the quays. For nearly a hundred years Southampton experienced what was nevertheless to prove only a transient rise to prominence as a fashionable seaside-resort-cum-spa that in its heyday almost rivalled Bath and Brighton. Its waters were praised for their efficacy in curing 'tedious agues, black and yellow jaundice, schirrus of the spleen, scurvy, green sickness, paralytic disorders, etc.' and were declared to be an unfailing remedy for barrenness in women. In addition to baths, new assembly rooms, a playhouse, banks and a newspaper came into existence; coffee-rooms and circulating libraries competed with each other; and many townsfolk fitted up their houses 'in the neatest and genteelest manner' to provide accommodation for the visitors. Coach services increased in number and gradually in speed, and a thickening fringe of gentlemen's seats appeared on the north of the town and to the east across the Itchen, while the road over the Common was planted with trees that grew into the splendid avenue which is still there to-day. New sports and pastimes developed; in particular archery with headquarters at an Archers' Lodge that afterwards gave its name to the modern Archers Road that debouches into London Road. Then as the spa declined and the coming of steam in the 1840s brought in the era of docks and railways this period merged into that which saw the development of the modern port.

Meanwhile the physical expansion of the town, governed by its peninsular position, had at first mainly taken two directions and shown two different characters. Before the end of the eighteenth century the once fashionable districts behind the old High Street had sunk in the social scale and were becoming slums; while Above Bar, as the street and district north of Bargate were called, came to rank as the genteel part of the town. Here in the early nineteenth century there developed a northward thrust of successive residential areas marked by much good Regency building. Eastward and north-eastward, however, there was another expansion that was chiefly artisan and industrial, linking the district of St Mary's more closely to the old town on one side and on the other joining it to Northam on the banks of the Itchen. This formerly separate little port was becoming an industrial suburb by the 1850s, with kilns, foundries, developing shipbuilding and marine engineering trades, gasworks, working-class houses and small shops. More directly to the east of the old town the coming of the railway and the docks had led to the rapid urbanisation of the area around the Terminus or Docks Station (now disused), which soon drew to itself more and more of the commercial bustle that had formerly centred about the old Town Quay at the foot of the High Street. In the second half of the century the northward expansion divided to creep round the Common on either side, aided by the break-up and sale for building purposes of the estates surrounding the large mansions that had fringed the town in this direction. Streets of suburban houses stretched out to take in the former village of Portswood to the north-east, which in turn began to spread northwards towards Swaythling and uphill by way of rurally-named Highfield to the eastern and north-eastern verges of the Common. On the north-west of the town an extension of boundaries in 1895 took in the former villages of Shirley, Freemantle and Millbrook, themselves much grown; while to the east the building of Cobden Bridge in 1883 furthered the growth of Bitterne on the other side of the Itchen and paved the way for its twentieth-century absorption along with Woolston, Sholing and other more outlying areas.

Southampton may thus be broadly said to have experienced since the Norman Conquest three periods of prosperity and one of decline. To this must be added that the third and most striking of these prolonged periods of prosperity was brutally but relatively briefly interrupted by the shattering blows which the town received from more than 50 air-raids during the Second World War. For a few years afterwards it seemed stunned and half-ruined. Then from the early 1950s a remarkable renaissance began which went beyond a mere restoration of its former

4   Opposite *Lymington: a glimpse of Three Quay Hill with its pavement of setts and its cheerful bay-windowed cottages.*

state and has carried it far towards becoming a regional capital for central southern England, up-to-date, attractive and splendidly equipped. While continuing till lately to be a vast ocean passenger port, it has also become an important cargo centre whose quays accommodate the world's largest container ships, as well as a prominent terminal for air, road and rail transport and the scene of an architectural revolution which has made it (to quote Mr David Lloyd in *The Buildings of Hampshire*) 'more than most provincial cities, a place to come to for modern architecture'.

These vicissitudes are reflected in its buildings, which date chiefly from these three prosperous eras; the Middle Ages, the spa period in the later eighteenth and early nineteenth centuries, and then the later nineteenth and the twentieth, culminating in the architectural achievements of the last 15 or 20 years.

Most of the medieval remains, in which the main architectural interest of the city probably still lies, are naturally within the old walled town, which presents perhaps the most impressive example of medieval urban defence in England. It is true that the circuits of the walls of York and Conway are more nearly complete, but they have less varied interest than Southampton's, whose defences contain work of many different periods. The walls, nearly a mile and a quarter of which survive, are still lined by many towers, the names of some of which, such as Catchcold and Windwhistle at the north-west corner, reflect the conditions under which generations of watchmen must have looked out in all weathers. The finest section is an arcaded and machicolated stretch of the fourteenth-century western wall, into which the seaward walls of pre-existing stone houses were incorporated and against whose base the waters used to lap at high tide, continuing to do so till the twentieth-century reclamations of land from the foreshore that made possible the building of the New Docks and of much else besides. Four of the medieval gates still stand, though there is no other (and can never have been, in Southampton) to touch the Bargate on the north. This is probably the finest town gateway in the country, despite the incongruous addition to its inward face in 1809 of a statue of George III, clad even more incongruously in Roman costume; and notwithstanding the demolition in 1932-7, after a generation of complaints about the obstacle it presented to traffic, of the parts of the walls on either side in order to create a roundabout. This has left the gate, as has been somewhat caustically said, looking like a huge piece of stage

5   Opposite: *New Forest ponies grazing in a sunny glade.*

scenery, 'a sort of medieval Arc de Triomphe in an insipid twentieth-century setting'. In later medieval days the upper floor of the Bargate became the town's guildhall, and afterwards in more modern times its first museum.

Neither the West Gate, though in 1415 an army marched through it to embark at the West Quay for the campaign that led to Agincourt, nor God's House Gate at the south-eastern corner of the walls is imposing; while the Blue Anchor postern (so named in rather later days from a neighbouring tavern) never had more than minor significance. God's House Gate derived its name from the nearby Domus Dei or God's House, an almshouse and hospice for travellers, founded in 1185 by a rich merchant. The hospice was abolished at the Reformation, but the almshouse, which was rebuilt in 1861, and its chapel which was carefully restored at the same time remain. The latter was taken over at the end of the seventeenth century by a congregation of French Huguenots fleeing from Louis XIV's persecution of Protestants, who a generation or so later joined the Church of England. The French Church, as it was called, continued to be used regularly till 1939, and a service according to the Anglican Prayer Book in French is still occasionally held in it. In the early fifteenth century God's House Tower, much larger than most of those included in the walls, was built at the end of a spur projecting from the gate, in order to guard the sluice controlling the flow of water into the town ditch outside the walls. At the end of the eighteenth century the eastern part of this ditch was converted into the first section of an abortive canal that was constructed to join the Redbridge-Andover Navigation at the former place at the head of Southampton Water, with the object of opening up water communication with Salisbury. Since barges were already being worked between Southampton and Redbridge along the Water, it was highly debatable whether this canal running closely parallel to it was needed, and an anonymous rhymester satirised it in these lines:

> *Southampton's wise sons found their river so large,*
> *Tho' 'twould carry a ship, 'twould not carry a barge;*
> *But soon this defect their sage noddles supplied,*
> *For they cut a long ditch to run close by its side.*
> *Like the man who contrived a hole in his wall,*
> *To admit his two cats — the one large, t'other small —*

When a great hole was cut for great puss to go through,
Had a little one cut for little cat too.

The canal never paid its way and traffic ceased within four years from its opening in 1802, but its memory is preserved in the name of Canal Walk, given to the lane that ran along the first section of its line after it was filled in. A parallel lane on the inner side of the eastern wall still bears the more ancient name of Back-of-the-Walls; while in recent years God's House Tower has been converted into an excellent archaeological museum that amply repays a visit.

A few fragments of the castle still stand, notably part of the north-east bailey wall (though now pierced to give access to a car-park) and the bases of the towers that flanked its eastern gate, which were uncovered and restored when the ring road was made. In addition to the remains of the stone houses already mentioned those of another are concealed behind the sadly bogus front of the Red Lion Hotel in the High Street. This has a Norman cellar and chimney-breast and a fine and lofty if somewhat tricked-out hall traditionally supposed to have been the scene of the trial of the conspirators against Henry V in 1415 ('The Southampton Conspiracy'), though no documentary evidence for this has been found. The most important medieval commercial buildings still standing are the fourteenth-century Wool House (largely rebuilt) at the foot of French Street which was originally used for storing wool before shipment and has now been splendidly restored as a maritime museum, and the Weigh House in French Street – the shell of a building where the royal weigh-beam was kept, but which was badly damaged in the wartime blitz.

Of medieval church architecture comparatively little survives. St Michael's, with its early Norman tower, its font of black Tournai marble and two medieval brass lecterns, is the only parish church of this period left intact by the air-raids. It was probably built immediately after the Norman Conquest – St Michael being the patron saint of Normandy – as the place of worship of the new French settlers in the town. One of the lecterns, considered perhaps the most beautiful in England, belonged originally to Holy Rood church in the High Street, from whose blitzed ruins it was rescued in 1941. This latter church, originally fourteenth-century but largely rebuilt in early Victorian days, has been left a shell but tastefully converted into a memorial to merchant seamen, including, as a plaque on the west wall recently transferred from another site records, those who lost their lives in the sinking of the mammoth White Star liner *Titanic* in 1912. The officers and crew of this ill-fated leviathan, lost on her maiden voyage by a collision with an iceberg, were mainly Southampton men; and her engineer officers, who were almost entirely drawn from the town and who remained below at their posts until the end in order to keep her afloat a little longer and give others more time to take to the boats, are commemorated by a special monument in East Marlands Park. There was also an Augustinian priory of St Denys in what was then the country well outside the town though the district to which it gave its name is now deeply embedded in it; but of this priory nothing now remains except a fragment in a garden in Priory Road and a small archway re-erected in the Tudor House Museum.

Comparatively little building survives in Southampton from the years between 1500 and about 1770. The Tudor House in St Michael's Square which has just been referred to would be the outstanding contribution from the beginning of this period if it is not to be reckoned late medieval, as perhaps it should be since it might have been built as early as 1491 and in any case incorporates a banqueting-hall which may be at least a century older. The High Street, praised by the traveller John Leland in the 1540s when it was mainly timber-fronted as 'one of the finest streets in any town in England', retained something of this reputation in later centuries when it abounded in bow-windows and indeed until much of it was wrecked by bombs in the 1940s. Unfortunately not a great deal of its post-war reconstruction has any architectural pretensions, though the part between the shell of Holy Rood church and the Bargate still keeps a little of its pre-war distinction. For the early eighteenth century there is Nicholas Hawksmoor's South Stoneham (manor-) House, two miles north-east of the old walls but now within the city limits and converted into a hall of residence for the University with the addition of an ultra-modern seventeen-storey tower block that has been skilfully added without detriment to the old house or even to its setting.

For the spa period much mainly domestic architecture remains, though the blitz and the post-war developments between them destroyed a good deal. What survives is rather widely scattered; and indeed it was an architectural weakness of Regency and early Victorian Southampton that it never had the consistent character of Cheltenham or the impressiveness of parts of Brighton, both of which and especially the former were built more at one period and in one piece. A reason for the disjointedness of Regency Southampton is that at this moment in the town's northward development up the peninsula between the Test and the Itchen it had to overleap the common fields that lay on both sides of the ribbon development Above Bar. The effect was that the town's late Georgian growth was bisected and much of it thrown to the north of these commons, where it survives rather incompletely in Carlton Crescent, Rockstone Place, Bedford Place, Cumberland Place and Brunswick Place. The most ambitious project of the spa period in this area failed, however. In the heyday of the period it was felt that Southampton ought to have something as distinctive as Bath's Royal Crescent or Tunbridge Well's Pantiles, and a plan was therefore formed which collapsed after a promising start, for building a Polygon of 12 large houses with gardens tapering inwards to a central block comprising a hotel, assembly rooms and shops. The site of the project is now occupied by a luxurious modern hotel which has usurped its name.

Within the old walls some buildings of the spa period survive: the Dolphin Hotel in the High Street, as rebuilt in the 1770s (the best eighteenth-century structure in the city); its neighbour the Star, which still preserves a notice carved in the stonework of its gateway – 'Coach to London, Sundays excepted, Alresford, Alton. Performs ten hours'; the former Yacht Club at the bottom of Bugle Street and some other houses in that street. There is also a concentration near the disused Docks railway station but slightly antedating it, comprising Oxford Street and Queen's Terrace with some of their now rather dingy neighbours, representing a once fashionable residential quarter that sprang up here outside the walled town in the 1830s. The coming of the railway in 1840, however, with its terminus only a few yards from the bow-windows of Queen's Terrace, and then the building of the first docks not much further away and only a couple of years afterwards, soon changed the character of the district and made it a region of hotels, offices and bustle.

It was at roughly the same time as this that the town's nineteenth-century expansion northward and north-eastward transferred its urban centre of gravity from the High Street to Above Bar, which became the chief commercial thoroughfare. In the Second World War it was largely destroyed by bombing and its rebuilding occurred mostly in the 1950s before the city's renaissance had really gathered momentum, and hence took place in a rather commonplace fashion, save for one or two buildings. It has in fact been described by an eminent authority whose reaction to the city is otherwise distinctly complimentary as having 'the look that the main street of an otherwise up-and-coming Middle West town might have had in the 1930s if there had been planning control and Portland stone'. Very recently, however, that part of it to the immediate north of Bargate has been converted into a not unpleasing pedestrian precinct.

The Civic Centre (a name coined by Southampton and afterwards used extensively elsewhere) was built on the West Marlands in the 1930s to house the municipal administration, which for 150 years had been centred in, or latterly had been more and more squeezed into, a Georgian Audit House in the lower High Street that was destroyed in the blitz. More impressive in its scale than in its style, it has been called 'perhaps the most ambitious civic building erected in the provinces during the inter-war years, a symbol of Southampton's heyday as a port, prospering while much of the rest of the country was in the darkness of a slump'. Damaged during the air-raids but restored after the War, it is really a complex of buildings dominated by a tower 182 feet high that is the main landmark of the city. Besides the municipal administration it houses also the law courts, a fine art gallery better endowed than any other in the south of England which has soon attained a national reputation, and a central public library. The tower contains a peal of nine bells which four times daily play the tune of the well-known hymn 'O God our help in ages past', whose composer Isaac Watts was a native of the town and is commemorated by a statue in a nearby park that bears his name.

The architectural revolution which the city has undergone since about 1955 is manifest in a variety of impressive urban redevelopments, the most outstanding of which are the Holy Rood Estate to the east of the shattered church of that name, probably the best post-war rehousing scheme in the city with its pleasingly proportioned four- and nine-storey blocks; the transformation of the inner part of Northam, once the city's nearest approach to a slum area, by another striking rehousing scheme whose centrepiece is the 16-storey Millbank Tower; and the 14-storey Castle House which occupies the site of the ancient keep and dominates the old town more surely than that can ever have done. In the suburb of Highfield the University has expanded its buildings rapidly to match its fast-growing number of students, under the guidance and largely to the design of Sir Basil Spence, who was responsible for the austere and dramatic Nuffield Theatre that is now its most distinctive feature. Many good commercial and other buildings have also arisen in various parts of the city during these years, and ancient and historic monuments such as God's House Tower and the Wool House have been excellently restored.

Nevertheless in spite of its renaissance and its prosperity Southampton has its problems. The seaborne passenger-traffic on which the port has depended so much for so long has latterly come under growing competition from air transport; and though the city's airport is a busy one, dealing annually with a quarter of a million passengers and $1\frac{1}{2}$m. kilos of freight by means of services to the chief cities of the British Isles as well as to Paris, Brittany and Spain, it is far from being in the front rank of international air transport. And while the cross-Channel ferries still take increasing number of passengers and cars to France, Spain, Portugal and North Africa, the great expansion in foreign travel by air has reduced drastically the total number of passengers carried by sea. A limited solution, or rather palliative, for the decline in liner traffic has been the diversion of passenger liners to holiday cruises, especially in winter-time when they are less in demand for direct transport, particularly on the North Atlantic route. But the port's salvation — and something more than merely that — has proved more and more to be the great and rapid shipping revolution here which has largely replaced the ocean-going liners by the oil tankers and giant container vessels that berth at the container terminal which has made Southampton the country's largest port outside London.

TWO

North to Winchester

Two roads lead from Southampton to Winchester, with another short secondary one between them which runs from the suburb of Swaythling as far as the western outskirts of the railway town of Eastleigh two or three miles distant. On its way this passes North Stoneham, which is now no more than a church and a former park, since the Regency house in which lived the Fleming family who had flourished in south Hampshire since the Norman Conquest has long been demolished. The church is worth a visit, since besides the mural tablet to the Slavonian oarsmen already mentioned it contains other interesting monuments. In particular there is the large tomb of Sir Thomas Fleming, who became Lord Chief Justice in the time of James I, having previously as Chief Baron of the Court of Exchequer given a decision in the famous Bate's Case in favour of the King's right to levy 'impositions' or additional customs duties in order to augment his revenue. There is also an elaborate wall-monument to Admiral Lord Hawke, who lived at the Grange at Swaythling, which has a detailed rendering of his great victory over the French at Quiberon Bay in 1759.

The Itchen valley road to Winchester plunges straight into Eastleigh, a parvenu town that has virtually supplanted the much older village of Bishopstoke on the other side of the river. A railway station called at first Bishopstoke Junction was built here on the London & South-Western line when a branch was opened in 1842 to Gosport, a branch that for a time served Portsmouth also, since until 1847 that town had no railway of its own. A village of railway workers then grew up here, taking its name from a neighbouring farm, and developed into a town after the L.S.W.R.

moved its carriage works to it from Nine Elms in London in 1891 and its locomotive workshops a few years later. After the First World War other industries appeared and the borough now has a population of over 40,000. Only the careful maintenance of a green belt keeps it separate from Southampton.

Crossing to the east bank of the river, the road to Winchester passes Brambridge House, which once belonged to Walter Smythe, the father of Mrs Fitzherbert who secretly married George III's son the Prince of Wales, afterwards Prince Regent and then King George IV. Here she spent much of her youth, though the legend that the marriage took place in the little Roman Catholic chapel in the nearby hamlet of Highbridge is unfounded. A couple of miles further on the road comes to Twyford, which has two notable houses. At Seager's Buildings the future poet Pope was at school and was expelled from it for writing a lampoon on the master; while at Twyford House Benjamin Franklin wrote most of his autobiography while staying with a friend. Beyond Twyford the road crosses the Winchester bypass that stems from the other or main Southampton road and then goes on to join this one.

This other and major highway to Winchester leaves Southampton by way of Bassett, passing at first through the remains of the thick woodlands that once sheltered the town on the north. As it does so, it throws off a road on the left to Romsey that goes by Chilworth, a well-to-do and outlying suburb with large houses among the woods as well as an unremarkable and modern manor-house that has been converted, like South Stoneham, into a hall of residence for the University. It also possesses a pretty church with a Norman font and the oldest bells in Hampshire. As this Romsey road leaves Chilworth and emerges from the woodland to descend a long and gradual slope to North Baddesley, the country opens out, revealing far-stretching vistas of rolling downland to the north and west. Most of North Baddesley is a conglomeration of twentieth-century housing and industry, but it has a delightful church in rural seclusion and opposite it a manor-house that was the successor of a medieval preceptory of the Knights Hospitallers. This order, originating from a hospital founded at Jerusalem in crusading times for the relief and aid of pilgrims, had branch houses throughout Europe dedicated to the same kindly care of these and other wayfarers. Their preceptory at North Baddesley was their headquarters in Hampshire until it was suppressed by Henry VIII.

After this branch to Romsey the main Winchester road dips to Chandler's Ford, which is to all interests and purposes a detached suburb of Southampton, and then skirts the grounds of Cranbury Park, an interesting and internally beautiful house not normally open to visitors. Here Sir Isaac Newton lived for the last years of his life with his half-niece (who was also his adopted daughter) and her husband; but the present house or much of it was built, probably in the 1790s, by the architect George Dance the younger, whose father built the Mansion House in London, for his brother Sir Nathaniel Dance-Holland. Afterwards the road passes through the once attractive village of Otterbourne, where Charlotte Yonge, the squire's daughter whose now almost forgotten novels were among the best-sellers of her day, lived for most of the nineteenth century. In all she wrote 160 books, many of them with a historical bias and one of which, *The Heir of Radclyffe,* went through 22 editions in 23 years. The profits of these works she devoted to supporting missionary activity and other charities. She also taught in the village Sunday school for 71 years and expounded the Bible in the day school for most of that time, and is buried in the churchyard near the granite cross which commemorates John Keble, one of the apostles of the Oxford Movement of Victorian days, who was vicar of the neighbouring parish of Hursley and by whom her views were much influenced; so much so indeed that she became the mouthpiece in fiction of his religious ideas.

A mile or two further on, the Winchester bypass turns off to cross the river, running close beneath St Catherine's Hill, which is crowned by an early Iron Age hill fort that was the first natural strong point of defence against an enemy advancing up the Itchen valley from Southampton Water. Excavations have shown that the fort, the predecessor and perhaps the progenitor of Venta Belgarum which developed on the lower ground across the river, was sacked in the first century B.C. and not reoccupied afterwards. Within its ramparts are the ruined foundations of a medieval chapel and also an ancient earthwork maze of the kind found at various places in England. These are usually turf-cut and situated on top of hills or downs, but their purpose is unknown. Some attribute a religious significance to them, while others think their object may merely have been to provide amusement at fairs. On the summit of the hill there is a clump of beech trees forming a landmark that can be seen from many miles around; and a mile or two onward the hamlet of Chilcomb nestles under the downs with its little Norman church.

From the point where the bypass leaves it the older road goes straight on to Winchester — dead straight, for here it is following the Roman road from Clausentum to Venta. A mile or so from the centre of the city, but within its boundaries, it passes the Hospital of St Cross, founded in 1137 by Henry of Blois, grandson of William the Conqueror, brother of King Stephen and Bishop of Winchester, to house 'thirteen poor impotent men so reduced in strength as rarely or never to be able to raise themselves without the assistance of another'. After his time it fell into decline under absentee masters who appropriated much of the proceeds of its endowments, but was rescued in the early fifteenth century by Cardinal Beaufort, another great political bishop of the see who was likewise of royal blood, being Henry IV's half-brother. Beaufort also endowed a new foundation, the Almshouse of Noble Poverty, which might be translated as being for decayed old gentlemen, though most of the first beneficiaries seem to have been his own retainers. Both De Blois's and Beaufort's pensioners can sometimes be seen in the streets to-day, De Blois's wearing a black gown with a silver Jerusalem cross and Beaufort's a claret-coloured robe and badge. In early- and mid-Victorian days the Hospital again became notorious for irregularities in its administration under an absentee master who was himself a son of a former bishop of Winchester, and before it was reformed it furnished the material for Anthony Trollope's satirical novel *The Warden*. An ancient Wayfarer's Dole of bread and ale which for 800 years has been provided for foot-travellers as part of the relief of the poor can still be obtained by those who apply for it (irrespective now of their means of transport), but only in tiny token quantities. Of the original buildings of the Hospital virtually nothing remains, but the church, built in the twelfth and thirteenth centuries, is one of the finest specimens of transitional Norman architecture in England.

Winchester, architecturally the richest of all English cathedral cities, came into being shortly before Roman times at an important crossing of the Itchen where it breaks through the downs and has since spread up them to east and west. The existence of this pre-Roman settlement meant that its Romano-British successor Venta had what may be called a flying start over some of the other provincial towns of Roman Britain and hence was larger and more important than many of them. Its walls enclosed an area of 138 acres; and indeed those of the later medieval city were largely a refaced version of them with part of the Roman work surviving on the eastern side. Recent excavations have brought to light traces of Venta's street-plan and of several buildings. From it five main roads radiated out, and the majority of the villas that are known to have existed in the county were situated within 15 miles of it.

The circumstances under which the Romans abandoned Venta and the Saxons occupied it are lost in the darkness that covers more than 200 years after the beginning of the fifth century. Even after that very little is known of it in the early Saxon era except that soon after Christianity reached what can now be called Winchester in the middle of the seventh century its first cathedral, known later as the Old Minster, was built. Then in the tenth century a second church called the New Minster arose close to it and the Old Minster was reconstructed. To it were then transferred the bones of St Swithun, a notable ninth-century bishop to whom together with the Holy Trinity and Saints Peter and Paul it was dedicated, but who had been a man of such humility that he had refused to be buried in it and had ordered his body to be merely interred in the churchyard. According to tradition the heavens wept so copiously on 15 July, the day when it was brought into the Old Minster to be reburied, and for 40 days afterwards that the legend arose and has persisted ever since that whenever it rains on that day it will continue to do so for this same period. After the Norman Conquest the Old Minster was pulled down to make way for a new cathedral, and a few years later the New Minster was transferred to a fresh site in the suburb of Hyde, where it remained, known as Hyde Abbey, until it also was demolished during the sixteenth-century dissolution of the monasteries. The exact original position of the two minsters in relation to each other and to their Norman successor, together with their foundations and ground-plans, have lately been revealed by archaeological work directed by Mr Martin Biddle.

Though rather surprisingly Winchester did not give its name to what in that case would probably have been known as Wintonshire to-day, its strategic situation soon made it again the most important town in the shire and afterwards in Wessex, and then in a limited sense the capital of England when the kings of Wessex became its overlords. Its predominance survived the Norman Conquest, thanks to its position in the centre of a region that was itself central to that part of the south coast of England lying opposite the main continental dominions of the Norman and early Plantagenet kings; and it was only when they lost these lands to the kings of France that it gave place to London as the country's administrative capital.

The Norman cathedral was built during the reigns of William the Conqueror and his son William Rufus, and on its consecration the bones of St Swithun were again disturbed to be translated to it from the Old Minster. Soon afterwards the ill-famed Rufus was buried there beneath the central tower, but seven years later this crashed down in ruins upon his tomb, which was widely taken as a sign of Heaven's anger that an enemy of religion and the Church should have been so honoured. The tower was rebuilt and the tomb later removed into the choir. Long afterwards, in 1868, it was opened and found to contain, besides the remains of what had certainly been a middle-aged Norman of high rank, two pieces of iron and some fragments of a long wooden shaft which were presumed to be all that was left of the arrow with which he had been mysteriously slain in the New Forest and which is known to have been buried with him.

The first major alteration to the cathedral, apart from the rebuilding of the tower, was made about 1200 by Bishop de Lucy, who rebuilt the previously apsidal (i.e., round-ended) eastern part behind the high altar in order to provide more accommodation for the many pilgrims who came to St Swithun's shrine there. The present retro-choir and Lady Chapel were thus brought into existence. This was followed in the fourteenth century by an undertaking which produced the most splendid transformation in the cathedral's history, when the west front and the nave were reconstructed. This mighty work, begun by Bishop Edington and completed by his successor William of Wykeham, imparted grace and light to the nave, gave it an added sense of height, and made it one of the greatest glories of Winchester, challenging comparison with the nave of any other cathedral in the world.

Since the city lies in a hollow, and the cathedral, though one of the longest in Europe, has no soaring spire and only a rather squat though massive central tower, no dramatic distant views of it are possible. Nevertheless it dominates the panorama of the city, which is seen at its best from St Giles's Hill on the eastern outskirts. It was on this hill that throughout the Middle Ages one of the greatest fairs in Europe was held annually, to which people flocked from many countries, most of them landing at Southampton and coming on from there.

Considerable as William of Wykeham's contribution to the cathedral by his part in the rebuilding of the nave had been, his greatest achievement and monument was the school he founded. Earlier schools in England, even those which like St Peter's at York drew some of their scholars from further afield than the place in which they were situated, had been appendages of churches or cathedrals. Wykeham made his an independent foundation, the sole reason for whose existence was the education of the boys, and thus provided the model for the public schools of later ages and in particular for Eton 50 years afterwards. Moreover he was the first founder to have a coherent idea of a system of tuition rising from school to college, for in his wish to have an educated clergy who could repair the ravages made in their ranks by the Black Death he designed his foundation at Winchester to be the feeder of the New College at Oxford which he had already established, though it was to remain quite independent of it in government. He also instituted the idea of internal discipline being largely maintained by the boys themselves – the prefectorial system which still prevails in English schools. It must be admitted, however, that the subtle charm of the buildings is rather marred by the reticence and even austerity of the approach through the somewhat sunless College Street; especially if that is reached from the contrasting cathedral close with its happy variety of building styles and through the charming fourteenth-century Kingsgate, one of the city's two surviving gates, which has the tiny church of St Swithun perched on top of it.

The oldest of the College buildings, completed by the time that Wykeham died in 1404, are the Outer and Chamber Courts with their respective gatehouses, the Chapel and Hall at the far end of the Chamber Court, and the Cloister or Cemetery beyond. Additions were made in the fifteenth century, and many afterwards. The actual School is a detached late seventeenth-century building close to the Cloister, which has been attributed without any reputable authority to Sir Christopher Wren. The other cloister, more than 500 years later in time, is one of the finest modern war memorials in the country. The work of Sir Herbert Baker, it is undoubtedly one of his best buildings. The badges of the corps in which the fallen Wykehamists served are blazoned on the roof, and in the floor at the gateway into the Meads there are four stones from the ruins of Ypres. The College Library is rich in book craftsmanship of many periods and contains a remarkable Empire Clock in Baker's style with two dials, the inner being a twelve-hour clock and the outer marking twenty-four hours and showing the time at Greenwich and in various parts of what was still the Empire when it was made, the several time zones being indicated by symbols such as South Africa's springbok and Canada's maple leaf.

Several of the medieval bishops of Winchester were like Wykeham men of great mark in the land in an age when not merely learning but also administrative gifts were mainly confined to the clergy. The greatest was probably that Henry of Blois already mentioned, who built a fortress-palace for himself within the walls at Wolvesey between the cathedral and the river, of which only ruins remain. It was replaced in Charles II's reign by a newer episcopal palace also allegedly built from a design by Christopher Wren, but most of this was pulled down a century or more later, leaving only one wing that faces these ruins across a green to form the Bishop's House of to-day.

At one time a royal castle which the Normans had built on the western hill near the fourteenth-century Westgate confronted the bishops' palace-castle across the city and was still strong enough to be the chief centre of Royalist resistance when Winchester was besieged by the Parliamentarians during the Civil War. When the city was finally taken by a force under Cromwell's own command a good deal of damage was done to the cathedral by the triumphant Puritan soldiery, though the townspeople successfully petitioned Parliament to cancel its original decision to pull it down. Nevertheless chantries were defaced, statues and choir-stalls mutilated and books and manuscripts trampled in the streets or thrown into the river. Wykeham's tomb escaped damage, however; tradition says because a Parliamentarian officer who had been a Wykehamist stood in front of it with drawn sword. The castle on the western hill was later demolished except for the Great Hall which passed into the hands of the county authorities, who used it as an assize court. On its wall hangs an immense round table that has been called King Arthur's, which it certainly is not, though it is equally certainly some centuries old.

When Winchester began to prosper again after the restoration of Charles II, the new king bought a site near the ruined castle from the

Corporation for the sum of five shillings. Here in 1683 a royal palace began to be built to a design which was genuinely Wren's, but when Charles died two years later work on the unfinished building was stopped and it was never used as a palace; perhaps fortunately, for by that time Wren had begun to turn from his earlier calm manner to the baroque flavour of his later style. Lord Torrington, indeed, afterwards called the uncompleted structure – though perhaps too sweepingly – 'a miserable deserted intention of Royalty' likely to have resulted in something 'unsightly, ill-situated' and 'without beauty or retirement'. In the eighteenth century it was used to house French prisoners-of-war and in 1796 became a barracks, which it has remained although largely destroyed by fire in 1894 and afterwards rebuilt. The present quite impressive buildings, of brick with stone dressings, therefore date from the beginning of this century.

To-day the barracks house the Rifle Depot of the Royal Green Jackets and the headquarters of the Light Division. The present composition of the famous Green Jackets regiment is the result of the amalgamation in 1966 of the Oxfordshire and Buckinghamshire Light Infantry (themselves the product of a much earlier amalgamation of the 43rd and 52nd Foot) with the King's Royal Rifle Corps (60th Rifles) and the 95th or Rifle Brigade, as the regiment's three regular battalions. At the end of the eighteenth century the 43rd and 52nd had been the first regiments to be trained as light infantry, and together with the 95th Rifles had constituted the famous Light Brigade which Sir John Moore organised and developed at Shorncliffe Camp after 1803. Renamed the Light Division, this became the spearhead of Wellington's army in the Peninsular War. The 60th had been raised in North America at the beginning of the Seven Years' War, and was composed of English settlers in the then American colonies (whose knowledge of the terrain and of Indian warfare contributed largely to the magnificent service the new regiment performed in that struggle), and of German and Swiss immigrants in Pennsylvania, which was the chief recruiting ground of the corps. They were commonly called the Royal Americans before the colonies broke away, and their green uniforms, adopted as more suitable for forest fighting than the traditional red coats of the rest of the army, were afterwards worn by all rifle regiments, giving rise to the nickname which has become an official designation. In 1858 the first rifle depot

6   Opposite *The north front of The Vyne, one of Hampshire's great houses. The fine portico built on to this splendid Tudor mansion by John Webb in the middle of the seventeenth century was the earliest of its kind on a country house in England.*

was established at the Winchester barracks as a training centre for the King's Royal Rifle Corps and the Rifle Brigade. In 1951 its name was changed to the Green Jackets' Depot, and then in 1958 to the Green Jackets' Brigade Depot when the Oxfordshire and Buckinghamshire Light Infantry were brigaded with these two rifle regiments; eight years after which the amalgamation of the three into a single regiment, already referred to, took place.

The county regiment, the Royal Hampshires, has so far succeeded in preserving its separate identity in spite of the recent changes, although for a time it was reduced to company strength. It was formed by the combination, as an outcome of the Cardwell reforms of 1881, of the 37th and 67th Foot, which had been raised in the eighteenth century and were later known during their separate existence as the North and South Hampshire Regiments respectively. It now forms part of the Prince of Wales' Division whose headquarters and depot are at Lichfield in Staffordshire, but has its own regimental headquarters in Winchester at Serles House in Southgate Street.

Near the Great Hall but on the other side of the main road and the Westgate impressive new county offices were built some years ago in a not unpleasing style, and more recently new law courts have been added to the east of the Hall. Another successful modern building and one that has survived a very testing confrontation is the Wessex Hotel which arose in 1961-3 across the Close from the cathedral. By keeping its scale down to that of the other buildings in the Close and using materials familiar to Winchester it has proved, in Sir Nikolaus Pevsner's words, that while employing the twentieth-century idiom without compromise it can stand up to the idioms of the past.

Nevertheless there might conceivably have been no such confrontation, for at the beginning of the present century it was realised that the eastern end of the cathedral was sinking in a bog. When Bishop de Lucy rebuilt it he had had to build on a waterlogged marsh and had made what for that day was a remarkably good artificial foundation of beech trunks that had borne their burden for 700 years but were now rotting and settling. These parts of the cathedral had consequently sunk more than two feet; walls and buttresses were leaning, arches distorted, great cracks showing and stones falling from the roof. Since the walls were in no condition to bear the vibration that would be caused by hammering and the marshy

7   Opposite above *Looking eastward from St Boniface Down in the Isle of Wight across Sandown Bay to Culver Cliff.*

8   Opposite below *The front and pier of the sheltered seaside resort of Ventnor at the foot of Boniface Down.*

foundations would not stand pumping dry, it was decided to underpin the building. This was done almost single-handed over a period of five years by a diver, William Walker, working under water and in darkness to lay bags of concrete on the gravel bottom below the marsh so that concrete blocks could then be built on them and pinned securely to the underside of the cathedral. Walker's name is still remembered in the annual St Swithun's day service, and there is a memorial to him on the west wall.

Not far outside the Westgate is an obelisk that commemorates the visitation of the city by the Great Plague of 1665-6, which smote it grievously in spite of a guard having been put on the gates to prevent infection being brought in. The monument, erected by a Charitable Society of Natives of Winchester founded to relieve those survivors of the pestilence whom it had left in distressed circumstances, was built on the base of a fifteenth-century processional cross on which while the plague was raging bowls of water mixed with vinegar were placed for townsfolk to drop money into in payment for the provisions which the country folk left nearby, not daring to enter the city. Not even the countryside was safe, however, for in the village (now a suburb) of Weeke on the Stockbridge road that turns north-westward outside the Westgate scarcely a soul was left alive.

The High Street of Winchester has been said to have a greater wealth of historical associations than any other street in England. The massive Westgate from which it is best to begin a walk down it, though preferably after climbing to its roof in order to get a view over the city perhaps second only to that from St Giles's Hill, is basically thirteenth-century though it has been much repaired and restored; and the little museum in the room above the gate is exceptionally interesting for its size. Branching from the street as one descends the hill are Jewry Street which was once the Jewish quarter and Parchment and Brook Streets which were the site of the binderies when Winchester was famous for its many beautiful manuscripts. Off the High Street too are Staple Gardens whose name betokens that this was once the centre of the wool market, and Southgate Street which was the jewellers' locality. Near it on the southern side is the Royal Oak Inn, built in 1630 but claiming that its subterranean bar is the oldest bar in the country – a claim disputed, however, by the Trip to Jerusalem at Nottingham and by several other inns. The bar's long, smooth and very well-worn shovehalfpenny table has been in use for two or three hundred years and is also claimed to be the oldest in the land.

A little lower down the High Street is Godbegot House, which derives its name (though its original meaning is doubtful and disputed) from an area of land that was known as the Manor of Godbegot when it formed part of King Ethelred the Unready's wedding present to his bride the Norman princess Emma. On her death she left it to the Priory of St Swithun attached to the cathedral, in whose hands and then those of the Dean and Chapter it remained for 800 years, independent of civic jurisdiction and forming for much of this time an alsatia or place of sanctuary where criminals could take refuge. In 1866 the Ecclesiastical Commissioners sold it to a private individual. The house itself is mainly sixteenth-century, especially on the long north side whose mighty timber frame and mellow brickwork can now be properly seen after the demolition of an obtrusive ironworks in 1957, but the façade fronting the High Street has been too much restored to be really interesting. Nearby but on the other side of the street stands the Butter Cross built early in the fifteenth century, on whose steps the marketwomen sold butter and other commodities. Sweepingly but ably restored by Sir Gilbert Scott in 1865, it is considered by many the most beautiful city cross in the country. Close beside it there are several striking old houses, with the covered shopping way called the Pentice beyond them; and nearby was the old meat market, the shambles off Fleshmonger Street that was the butchers' quarter. Then comes the former guildhall, now Lloyd's Bank, built in Queen Anne's time, with a great City Clock of the same period and in the niche below it a statue of that queen; and where the High Street widens at the bottom into the Broadway beyond this guildhall's Victorian successor, a gigantic and impressive – though purely imaginative – statue of Alfred the Great by Hamo Thorneycroft that was erected in 1901, the thousandth year after the king's death, looks down upon the city traffic.

From the foot of the High Street the City Bridge crosses the Itchen, and just upstream from it the City Mill bestrides the river. There has been a watermill here for many centuries, though not outstandingly active, since it was derelict for a long time before its rebuilding in 1744, after which it resumed its work of grinding corn till about 1900. After that it was reconditioned and given to the National Trust, which has let it to the Youth Hostels Association, so that it has become one of their most popular hostels. Further on again, at the foot of St Giles's Hill and on the corner of Chesil Street to the right, is an early sixteenth-century but carefully restored house called Chesil Rectory. Since Chesil, the name of this area, is derived from the Old English *cisil,* meaning shingle, it is presumed that when the Itchen was much wider than it is now there was a spit or beach of shingle at this spot.

THREE

The Centre

The five roads which radiated from Winchester in Roman times had linked it with Cirencester, Silchester, Portchester, Clausentum and Old Sarum (Salisbury). The first four of these are partly incorporated in the present roads to Andover, Basingstoke, the village of Morestead three or four miles south-east of the city, and Southampton; while that to Sarum may still be followed by lane, trackway and path for half-a-dozen miles over the downs nearly to Ashley, where there are a Norman church and an earthwork thought to be Roman though probably adapted from an earlier one. Nearing Ashley the track passes close to Farley Mount, the highest point (586 feet) in the Winchester area, where a monument commemorates a marvellous leap made by a horse and rider in 1733. On top of a very large Bronze Age barrow whose summit is approached by a spiral path there is a little brick-and-plaster spire with an inscription telling that a favourite hunter which once belonged to Paulet, a member of the St John family who then lived at Farley Chamberlayne close by, is buried in the barrow. When Paulet St John was out hunting one day he came so suddenly and fast upon a chalk-pit with a 250-foot drop that he had no time to avoid it and so let his horse take the leap, which it did safely. Renamed 'Beware Chalk-Pit', the horse with St John up won a race at the Winchester meeting on Worthy Down later in the year. From Farley Mount there is a fine view on all sides and in particular northward over 20 miles of rolling country to where a second range of downs forms the northern boundary of the chalk.

On the present road to Salisbury via Stockbridge and about four miles from Winchester is the park of Lainston House, a handsome eighteenth-century building occupying an older site, in whose private chapel a secret marriage took place in 1744 between Elizabeth Chudleigh, who is said to have been the original of Beatrix Castlewood in Thackeray's novel *Henry Esmond,* and Augustus Hervey, a lieutenant in the Navy and a grandson of the Earl of Bristol. The notorious Miss Chudleigh, who was a maid of honour and the reigning toast at the court of George II, had begun her career by fascinating the Earl of Bath and had then become the mistress of the Duke of Hamilton, whom she hoped to marry. She had met Hervey at the Winchester Races and probably become somewhat attached to him, but her chief reason for marrying him seems to have been a wish to spite Hamilton, whom she accused of neglect. However she soon repented of her choice after having a child by Hervey, and is said to have had the page in the Lainston register which recorded the marriage torn out. They then lived apart for twelve years, during which she caught the eyes of both George II and Frederick the Great, the latter of whom much admired her ability to put away two bottles of wine at a sitting. Since it was now probable that Hervey would become Earl of Bristol, which in fact he presently did, she compelled the Lainston clergyman who had celebrated the marriage, and who was now dying, to make a fresh entry in the church register. But after becoming the mistress of the Duke of Kingston (she did everything by twos – dukes, monarchs, marriages and bottles of wine) she prevailed on him to go through a marriage ceremony with her and so made it necessary to tamper with the Lainston register once more, this time to delete the now unwelcome entry. However this was too much; the truth caught up with her soon after the Duke had died and left her his immense fortune, and she was tried before the House of Lords for bigamy and found guilty. Nevertheless she was let off lightly, though with a warning that she might find herself branded with a hot iron if she gave any further trouble. Bristol was unable to divorce her, since there was some evidence of his collusion in the bigamy, and she was left in possession of the Duke's fortune. With it she went to Russia, where she got on well with Catherine the Great, who had certain tastes in common with her; and then to France where she bought a royal palace, rejected a proposal of marriage from a Polish prince, and continued her career of love-affairs until she died at the age of 68. Bristol had died nine years before as an admiral who had seen much not strikingly distinguished service.

To the roads radiating from Winchester that have already been mentioned must be added those to Romsey in the Test valley, Petersfield and Alresford, this last both directly and by the winding upper valley of the Itchen. The road to Romsey passes near the ruins of Merdon Castle, built in the twelfth century by Bishop Henry of Blois, less as a fortress than as an episcopal palace to match Wolvesey within the walls of Winchester. In the fourteenth century, however, it was allowed to fall into disrepair, and little of it now survives except some lengths of wall seven feet thick. A mile further on the road comes to Hursley, where in the former manor-house Oliver Cromwell's amiable and colourless son Richard, who for a brief space succeeded him as Protector, lived till the restoration of Charles II forced him to flee abroad. After twenty years, however, it was realised that 'Tumbledown Dick' was so harmless that he could not possibly be a threat to the restored Stuarts, and he was allowed to come back to England. To recover his Hursley estate, however, he had to go to law with his own grasping daughters, though he succeeded in time to be buried there in 1712. The daughters then sold the estate to the Heathcote family, who pulled down the old Tudor house and built the nucleus of the present one; and it was the last of this family to reign there as squire who presented his former tutor John Keble with the living. The present church was built by Keble out of the royalties from his book, *The Christian Year*. The estate is now owned by I.B.M. and the house has become the centre of a complex of their offices and laboratories.

About a mile to the west of the still traceable Roman road from Winchester to Portchester and seven miles almost due south of the city is Marwell Hall, a remarkable early case of Tudor revival. About 1816 a new owner, William Long, harmoniously refashioned a manor-house which had itself been rebuilt from a medieval predecessor by Sir Henry Seymour, a brother of both Jane Seymour who was Henry VIII's third wife and Edward Seymour who became Duke of Somerset and Lord Protector of the Realm under their son Edward VI. With its low-pitched gables, Renaissance windows and solar or ladies' retiring-room, the house still looks much as it must have done in Seymour's time. It is one of two in Hampshire (the other being Bramshill) of which the 'mistletoe bough' legend is told, of a bride who in a game of hide-and-seek during her wedding festivities hid in a massive chest whose lid she was unable to reopen and in which her companions never thought of looking for her, so that she perished. Very recently the present owner has converted the grounds into a zoological park which contains a major collection of animals most of whom are living in as natural an environment as possible, both they and the visitors enjoying relative but separate freedoms. The house itself is not open to the public and can only be approached through this park.

The Petersfield road from Winchester climbs up out of the city to pass in a mile or two by Cheesefoot (or Chesford) Head, which at 579 feet almost disputes the primacy of Farley Mount and commands a similar but even more magnificent view, enhanced by a striking valley at its feet known to Wykehamists as the Amphitheatre and to others as Temple Valley. Four or five miles further on the road skirts the village of Cheriton, near which in 1644 was fought a battle of considerable importance in the Civil War, when the victory of the Parliamentarians under Sir William Waller over Sir Ralph Hopton's Royalist army checked the latter's threatening advance towards London from the south-west. Although Waller was called by the contemporary historian Clarendon 'a right good chooser of vantages', Hopton, who was his friend in private life, at first managed to outgeneral him; but over-confidence and bad discipline led the Royalist horse to charge down too soon from a slope which they had occupied, thus exposing themselves to a telling fire from Waller's guns and then a counter-charge by his cavalry. Hopton's main body tried to come to the rescue of their horse, but only became involved in their rout, though by a desperate rearguard action he succeeded in getting part of his army away. Out of ten or eleven thousand men engaged on either side a total of about two thousand fell.

Soon after skirting Cheriton the Petersfield road passes a lane on the right leading in less than half a mile to' Hinton Ampner, a hamlet consisting of a classic grouping of manor-house, church, rectory, a farmhouse or two and a cluster of cottages. As the name Hinton, from the Old English *hea-tun* – 'village on high ground' – implies, it stands high on the northern slope of a long ridge that stretches away eastward for some miles but to the westward soon falls gently towards the source of the Itchen. The suffix Ampner, which is a corruption of almoner, derives from the fact that when during the Middle Ages it was one of the Bishop of Winchester's manors it was appropriated to the office of the almoner of St Swithun's Priory to defray his expenses, and indeed in some old documents was simply called Prior's Hinton.

The present manor-house is the fifth or sixth to stand on this spot. During the Priory's tenure of the manor there seems to have been a small house here which is thought to have been burnt down early in the sixteenth century. It was succeeded by a Tudor house which survived until late in the eighteenth century, but was latterly reputed to be haunted. The manifestations or alleged manifestations came to a head while the house was occupied by a Mr and Mrs Ricketts to whom it had been let – perhaps for this reason – by its owners the Stawell family. Doors were heard opening and shutting at dead of night, and though the first and most natural explanation was that the servants were misbehaving a careful investigation by Mr Ricketts ruled this out. Other strange and disturbing noises were heard which presently included human voices and shrieks, and the servants for their part reported seeing strange figures which may have been the products of their over-excited imaginations. In 1771 Mrs Ricketts's brother, Captain John Jervis, afterwards to be the famous Admiral Earl St Vincent – a title which he won by his great victory over the Spanish fleet off the cape of that name – came to visit her. Pooh-poohing all supernatural explanations, he at once determined to sit up all night with a friend for several nights in succession in order to catch the miscreants he was convinced must be responsible. When on the first night they heard sounds of footsteps and banging doors he and his friend rushed out with their pistols in their hands but could find nobody and nothing to account for the phenomena. Captain Jervis insisted, however, that his sister and her family should leave the house as soon as possible, and it apparently remained almost deserted except perhaps for the ghosts. No explanation of the mystery was ever found, and since the house was virtually uninhabitable the owner decided in 1793 to pull it down and rebuild on a fresh and somewhat more sheltered site about sixty yards to the south. During the demolitions a box containing a small skull was found under one of the floors and was immediately removed by the steward, which did not prevent the news of the find from leaking out and being taken as proof of a story that had long circulated in the neighbourhood that the ghosts were those of a former Lord Stawell and his sister-in-law and that the skull was that of a baby which had been the fruit of their illicit intercourse and which they had murdered.

The house built in 1793 passed with the marriage of the heiress of the

Stawells to the Dutton family, in whose hands its successors have remained. Described as a modest yellow brick box completely out of fashion by the middle of the nineteenth century, it was pulled down in its turn in the 1860s and replaced by what the present squire and historian of Hinton Ampner, Mr Ralph Dutton, who was born and grew up in it, has called a Victorian monstrosity which he hastened to alter radically when he inherited it in 1935. For this purpose he employed as architects the firm of Lord Gerald Wellesley (afterwards Duke of Wellington) and Mr Trenwith Mills. Ill-luck continued, however, for after the work had been handicapped and then the reoccupation of the house delayed by the Second World War, during which it housed the evacuated staff and pupils of a Portsmouth girls' school, it was largely destroyed by fire in 1960. Nevertheless the strong outer walls survived, as well as the Adam ceiling of the dining-room, and by 1963 it had been once more rebuilt by Mr Trenwith Mills.

The story of these vicissitudes has been delightfully and sensitively told in scholarly detail by Mr Ralph Dutton in another Batsford book to which I am greatly indebted.

A mile or so further along the Petersfield road comes Bramdean with a number of eighteenth- and early nineteenth-century houses and an attractive bow-windowed public-house; and another mile beyond it there is on the left-hand side of the road what to a hasty or uninstructed glance might seem to be an ancient stone circle but is in fact a hoax perpetrated by a local landowner in relatively modern days. On the right another lane leads up to Brockwood (formerly spelt Brookwood), a spacious mansion standing in a finely wooded park, with the remains of a Tudor predecessor in the shape of a tower and some outbuildings close beside it. Here the Indian philosopher Krishnamurti has recently opened an international and residential educational centre with the object of enabling students and staff to explore together the implications of his tenets and achieve a new approach to living through self-knowledge.

The main road then crosses the A32 from Fareham to Alton and runs on towards Petersfield with the tower of Privett church, 160 feet high, standing up on the ridge to the left. In a county remarkably rich in Victorian churches this is one of the most striking, resembling both inside and out a substantial town church rather than a village one. Ahead, when the watershed between the Meon and the eastward-flowing Sussex

Rother has been crossed, a vista of the main range of the South Downs presently opens up.

Some miles further back a northward turning off the Winchester-Petersfield road at Cheriton into another which winds past the many thatched cottages of this attractive village brings one in a couple of miles to Tichborne, from whose manor-house the traditional Tichborne Dole is still distributed. The legend behind this is that in the twelfth century Lady Marbella Tichborne, who had spent her life in caring for the poor, made a deathbed pact with her hard-hearted husband that as much land as she could circumambulate while a brand that he had seized from the fire continued to burn should be set aside to grow corn for the poor of the parish. With her last ebbing strength – so runs the tale – she managed to crawl round twenty-three acres in the time, and with her final breath pronounced a curse on the house of Tichborne if this dole should ever be discontinued. Be this as it may, after their descendant Sir Henry Tichborne, doubtless for greater convenience, had substituted in 1796 a gift of money to the Church for the former distribution of flour, misfortune began to dog the family's footsteps. In a single generation seven daughters but no sons were born; and when Roger, the heir to the estates, was reported lost at sea in the middle of the nineteenth century the house seemed to be heading for extinction. A famous disputed succession case now followed. It was never conclusively proved that Roger had in fact been drowned, though his ship was alleged to have sunk with all on board; and his mother, a Frenchwoman who cherished enmity against the rest of the family, was convinced that he was still alive. A butcher named Arthur Orton, born in Wapping but living in Australia, who had come into touch there with men who had known Roger Tichborne, now built up an amazing structure of fraud and falsehood on the strength of what he had learned from them and claimed to be the missing heir. When he came to Europe to see Roger's mother she recognized or professed to recognize him as her son; and since she died soon after swearing affidavits to that effect it remains unknown whether she was really deceived or merely influenced by her hatred for the Tichbornes. After a trial lasting 102 days the fraud was exposed; the 'Tichborne Claimant' was then put on further trial for perjury and sentenced to fourteen years' penal servitude. The nearest genuine heir had meanwhile succeeded and the Dole hastily resumed in its original form.

Two miles north of Tichborne is Alresford, but the entry into the little town from this direction is the least attractive of the possible approaches, and indeed amounts to slipping into it by a side-entrance. The direct road from Winchester, after leaving there by climbing St Giles's Hill, strikes almost straight across country to be joined by the Itchen valley road a mile from Alresford, after which it enters the town along a wide tree-lined avenue, and passing through it, goes on to Alton and towards London. Nevertheless the High Street which it forms, though wide and pleasant, is not Alresford's most noted and picturesque thoroughfare, for that distinction belongs to an older street that joins the modern main one at right angles from the north. This is the appropriately named Broad Street, which has been claimed to be the best in Hampshire, and from the bottom of which a fourteenth-century bridge leads to the original village still called Old Alresford. New Alresford, as the town is still sometimes also called though it is now far from new, was by origin a made town like the French *bastides* or fortress-towns that were built to guard against attacks from the medieval English territories in France and thus frequently bear the name of Villeneuve; though it was neither so elaborate as they usually were nor was it military in character but commercial. It was founded about 1200 by Bishop Godfrey de Lucy of Winchester, who built a dam across the little river Alre which is one of the headwaters of the Itchen, dug a reservoir alleged to have covered 200 acres (though the pond that now represents it measures only 30) and canalised the Itchen above Winchester in the hope of creating a great trade waterway through it to Southampton. The town, which at first consisted only of Broad Street, prospered enough to be considered in the fourteenth century one of the ten greatest wool markets in the country, but the industry afterwards declined and Alresford also suffered several devastating fires, one result of which is that it has few houses dating from before the eighteenth century.

In the manor-house of Old Alresford, built in the middle of the eighteenth century, lived the greatest of the admirals of that period, George Brydges (Lord) Rodney. A local legend which is almost certainly apocryphal and libellous credits or debits him with the building of most of the public-houses that line the village street on either side in order that on occasion he might tack from one to another on his way home.

The Itchen valley road from Winchester to Alresford leaves the A33 to Basingstoke after it passes Headbourne Worthy – where there is a

Saxon church with remains of a once remarkable rood – and then Kings Worthy. Turning right beyond the point where the Winchester bypass comes in again, it traverses the other two Worthys, Abbots and Martyr. The name of this last seems to be derived, not from any martyrdom, but from the fact that about 1200 it was held by Henri la Martre, or in Old French 'the marten', perhaps a nickname; while 'worthy' signified a homestead. Then comes Itchen Abbas, so called because it once belonged to an abbey which Alfred the Great's son and successor Edward founded at Winchester. It was a favourite holiday resort both of Charles Kingsley, who wrote *The Water-Babies* there, and of the Liberal statesman Lord Grey of Falloden, whose fishing-cottage was his cherished retreat from London for thirty years until its destruction by fire. Across the river is Avington Park which Cobbett in his *Rural Rides* called (though with his usual exaggeration) 'one of the very prettiest spots in the world', adorned by a lake that is an expansion of the Itchen and an eighteenth-century house that is a perfect period piece and once belonged to the dukes of Chandos, passing from them to the family of the poet Shelley.

At Itchen Stoke two or three miles up-valley from Itchen Abbas the Candover stream which is one of the headwaters of the Itchen comes in from the north. Its pleasant valley, winding through open and gently rolling country, contains several attractive villages, notably the three which bear its name: Brown Candover, Chilton Candover and Preston Candover. The second of these has a long avenue of yew trees which once led up to a house that was pulled down in the eighteenth century, and under the site of its also long-demolished church there is an underground crypt whose existence remained unknown for many years until it was rediscovered in the 1920s.

The Basingstoke road out of Winchester runs as straight as an arrow for its first ten miles and almost as straight (though thereabouts it diverges from the old Roman road) for the remaining ten. It offers little but a monotonous succession of ups and downs in its passage through rather lonely country, though after the first five miles it is crossed at Lunways Inn by an ancient trackway which has given its name to the inn and can be followed on foot westwards for some miles till it meets the A30 highway from Salisbury and the west to London. Another five miles beyond the Lunways Inn the road passes on the right hand Stratton Park, once a seat of the Russell family which holds the dukedom of Bedford. In

1800 the estate was sold to the banker Sir Francis Baring, who was of German extraction, his grandfather having been a Lutheran pastor at Bremen though his father had moved from there to become a clothmaker in Devon. Sir Francis, who showed a genius for finance, laid the foundations of the firm that was to become world-famous as Baring Brothers and became the chairman of the East India Company. After buying the Stratton estate he had the house rebuilt by the younger George Dance and it remained in his family till about 1930. Only its portico still survives, skilfully converted with its mighty Tuscan columns and its pediment into an adjunct to a house built in the 1960s in a contemporary style.

At his death in 1810 Sir Francis was acclaimed as the first merchant in Europe. His second son, who was a statesman as well as a financier, became Lord Ashburton and established a branch of the family at The Grange at Northington in the Candover valley. He particularly distinguished himself as Britain's representative in the successful settlement of a boundary dispute between the United States and Canada in 1842, in the course of which he was said to have 'spread a social charm over Washington and filled everybody with friendly feelings towards England'. His nephew Francis Thornhill Baring represented Portsmouth in Parliament as a Whig for nearly 40 years, held several Cabinet posts, and became Lord Northbrook and the father of a viceroy of India; while another descendant of the first Sir Francis, Evelyn Baring, brought yet another peerage into the family as Lord Cromer, became the maker of modern Egypt and in his day its effective ruler, and is buried at Bournemouth in what was Hampshire soil until that town was transferred to Dorset.

At Micheldever a couple of miles from Stratton and on the other side of the main road is a church with several Baring monuments by the famous sculptor Flaxman and a central octagon by Dance that is its most distinguished feature. In the churchyard lies another and earlier man of foreign origin who became a Hampshireman by adoption – Henri de Massu de Ruvigny. Ruvigny, as he is usually called, was a seventeenth-century Huguenot marquess who had two brilliant military careers; one in the French army in which he became aide-de-camp to the great Marshal Turenne, and one in the English service. Driven to England by Louis XIV's persecution of the Huguenots, he served his adopted country valiantly and well for 25 years, during which he lost an eye and an arm in battle and became a general and Earl of Galway. On one occasion he was taken prisoner by the French, but so great was the admiration his former fellow-countrymen felt for his military talents and his valour that instead of treating him as a traitor to France they hastened to release him. In his nobly-earned retirement he made his home at Rookley Manor, near Winchester, and was visiting a cousin at Stratton House when he died.

Some five miles or so beyond the Micheldever turning another on the left leads to the pleasant tucked-away village of North Waltham, and then to Steventon, where Jane Austen's father was rector and where she spent the first 25 years of her life. In a world limited to a few neighbouring villages and country houses linked only by bad lanes, and with no greater excitement than an occasional ball at Basingstoke, she wrote *Pride and Prejudice, Sense and Sensibility* and *Northanger Abbey* with all the assurance that came from a keen study of manners and a penetrating insight into character such as one might think that only a far wider experience of life could have produced.

FOUR

The Hamble and
Meon Country

It is a characteristic of most Hampshire rivers, including some of the shortest, that they broaden out into wide estuaries as they near the sea. Besides the Test which provides the major part of Southampton Water, this is true of the Hamble which enters it a few miles below Southampton. The Hamble rises little more than a dozen miles inland, on the southern fringe of the chalkland just north of Bishops Waltham where, as the name hints, an episcopal palace was built by – one almost says the inevitable – Henry of Blois in the twelfth century. With some alterations it continued as such until in the Civil War it was so thoroughly burnt by the Parliamentarians that it was afterwards allowed to fall into ruin. Such walls as still stand are mainly fifteenth-century in date, though they incorporate some of de Blois's stonework of three centuries earlier. Within their enclosure is a seventeenth- and eighteenth-century brick house which was recently the home of one of the greatest of the many great seamen who have taken their retirement in Hampshire – the late Admiral of the Fleet, Lord Cunningham of Hyndhope, an outstanding British naval figure of the Second World War. The town itself is a somewhat disappointing place whose older houses rather obviously need restoration, though the traffic problem caused till lately by the narrowness of its main streets and its many right-angled corners has now been eased by the building of a bypass.

Down-valley and south-west from Bishops Waltham is Hampshire's celebrated strawberry-growing district, an area where the soil is rich but the landscape and architecture are unremarkable. Its centre is Botley, also on the Hamble, a little town that has been attractive, with a surprising

9   Opposite above *Light and shade in Old Shanklin village.*
10   Opposite below *Godshill, probably the most attractive of the inland villages of the Isle of Wight.*

number of inns some of which are quite pleasing and one or two fine houses, but it is suffering now from a convergence of traffic. Here William Cobbett the Radical publicist lived and farmed from 1804 to 1817 at a now-vanished house called Fairthorn Farm whose gardens and outbuildings survive in the grounds of Botley Hill; and here he kept up a permanent quarrel with 'the Botley Parson', Richard Baker, whom he pilloried in his *Rural Rides.*

A mile or two below Botley the Hamble suddenly begins to widen out, and by the time the Southampton-Portsmouth road crosses it at Bursledon its estuary has developed and is dotted with cabin cruisers and other small craft. On the main road Bursledon is a mere piece of subtopia semi-detached from Southampton, but below the bridge it becomes a secluded village standing mainly though strangely aloof from the river on higher ground with its houses scattered almost casually around. By the riverside, however, it has a pleasant eighteenth-century inn, the Jolly Sailor. Warships were built here in the seventeenth and eighteenth centuries, and it now builds yachts.

As the river nears Southampton Water Hamble village and Warsash face each other on its west and east banks respectively. Hamble has been a yachting centre for decades past, thanks to the broad estuary; but like Hampshire itself it has a dual character, for the approach to it by land from Southampton reveals a side of it more concerned with aviation than sailing, for here there are aircraft factories and a College of Air Training. In its older parts, however, it is engagingly unselfconscious, and its uphill and winding main street has been likened by Sir Nikolaus Pevsner to a Devon or Cornish fishing village translated into Hampshire brick. Warsash for its part was once a very primitive crab-fishing hamlet, with a hinterland of heaths which was transformed after the middle of the nineteenth century into a warren of strawberry holdings. When yachtsmen discovered the Hamble in the early twentieth century there proved to be less scope for mooring on the Warsash side than on the other, and though Warsash now has a large and flourishing school of navigation which trains mercantile marine officers in well-constructed new buildings, it has only a few small boathouses. Being nearer the river-mouth than Hamble, however, it provides spacious views both of the yacht-filled estuary and out into the Solent.

Between Hamble and Woolston lies the suburban village of Netley,

11   Opposite above *Osborne House, once Queen Victoria's seaside home, designed by the Prince Consort.*

12   Opposite below *The entrance gateway of Carisbrooke Castle, where Charles I was for some time held captive after the Civil War.*

which used to be notable for three things, its abbey, its castle and its military hospital, of which only the first two survive. The ruins of the Cistercian abbey, founded as a daughter house of Beaulieu in Henry III's reign, have been preserved by the Ministry of Public Building and Works in such a way as to make them instructive and the site is an oasis of peace and calm. The castle was originally one of the forts constructed to defend the Solent in Henry VIII's later years, but was turned into a residence in 1627. Its tower, though it catches the eye from the water, was built only in the nineteenth century. The huge hospital, built immediately after the Crimean War in consequence of the exposure during it of the inefficiency of the Army's medical service, was architecturally a grandiose showpiece, but fell into desuetude and was demolished in 1966.

The river Meon, while not so long as the Test or the Itchen, whose right-angled course its own resembles, is at least twice the length of the Hamble but unlike it has no wide estuary. Rising in a combe of the main east-west ridge of mid-Hampshire downs, it descends to the delightful village of East Meon, through whose very pretty High Street it runs. But the glory of East Meon is its cruciform church, as fine as any village church in the county, lying so close below a perfect South Downs hill with smooth turf and no trees that it could not have a north aisle. With a twelfth-century central tower supported on four fine arches of the same period and with another of the county's black Tournai marble fonts, it is a veritable cathedral of the downs. Across the road from it is an early fifteenth-century courthouse dating from the time when the bishops of Winchester as lords of the manor sent their officer to hold court there.

At West Meon, an attractive village a couple of miles further on, the river turns southward. Here Thomas Lord, the groundsman of the Marylebone Cricket Club and creator of the most famous cricket ground in the world, spent the last two years of his life and was buried, though he was of Yorkshire birth and Scottish ancestry. An undistinguished public-house bears his name. The next in the string of comely villages in this favoured and fertile valley is Warnford, whose church, accessible by permission along a private path, has a Norman tower even more massive than East Meon's and a great Norman font. Close at hand but hidden by trees are the remains of a thirteenth-century hall miscalled King John's House but actually dating from about 1230. The old and narrow road that strikes upward from Warnford to Butser Hill over the downs that form the watershed between the Meon and the headwaters of the Sussex Rother was said by H. J. Massingham (who also declared that he would rather spend his last days in the Meon valley than anywhere else in England) to be unique in the country or even the world. As it goes on its way it skirts the spur that is puzzlingly called Old Winchester Hill, on which there are an Iron Age hill-fort and a fine set of bowl barrows. Why a hill that is more than a dozen miles away from Winchester should bear a name that would be better suited to St Catherine's Down, on whose summit there is the hill-fort that really could with some justice be called Old Winchester, is obscure. The Victoria County History's suggestion that the Romans, who also had a camp on the hill, may have found a similarity between it and Winchester, since at both a river breaks through a chain of hills, lacks conviction to say the least.

Across the valley from Old Winchester Hill the downland ridge continues with the equally lovely Beacon Hill; and another mile or so down-river from Warnford come three villages clustered so closely together as almost to form one: Corhampton, with a church that is pure Saxon except for the east wall of nineteenth-century brick that unfortunately faces the road; Exton, with a pleasant pub where in good weather one may take one's ease in the garden with the smooth translucent river rippling past one's feet; and Meonstoke, by whose church and pretty cottages it also runs. From Corhampton, too, there is a delightful 15-mile drive over the downs to Winchester; but by continuing down the valley one comes to Droxford near the border between the chalklands and the clay-and-sand country of south-east Hampshire. Here Izaak Walton, who married the rector's daughter, used to come fishing in the heart of the county which he said 'exceeds all England for swift, shallow,clear, pleasant brooks and store of trouts'. The village is full of pleasing domestic architecture, much of it modestly Georgian. Indeed the whole of the upper and middle valley of the Meon as it winds its way through these chalk downs is most attractive, and residence in these villages is much sought after by those who want rural peace.

It is now thought that the 'English' who settled in this valley after the breakdown of Roman rule were Jutes and not Saxons; and since the contemporary name for them, Meonwara, was Celtic it is also considered for that and other reasons that a considerable proportion of Celtic Britons may have survived among them, subordinated and more or less assimilated. 'More or less', since according to Mr Brian Vesey-Fitzgerald there are still throughout this area of hilly downs and narrow deep side-valleys two distinct types of people, dark and fair; the dark people being almost always quicker on the uptake than the stockier fair folk who are slower of speech and thought. They get on perfectly well together in work and play, and not many of either type will ever have heard of Jutes or perhaps even of Celts; but it is rare (he claims) for a 'mixed marriage' of the two types to occur. Be this as it may, it is certain that some of the more sophisticated of the darker type will sometimes make a pose or affectation of claiming to be Jutes by origin; and the dialect of the valley is said to be slightly different from that of other parts of Hampshire.

Just above Droxford a side-road to the left crosses the river and strikes south-westward over the downs for three miles to Hambledon. This village has repeatedly been called the home of cricket; and though the legend that the game was first played there must be discounted, since in some shape it was centuries older than the Hambledon Club, it may at least be claimed that it was there that the first club proper came into being, and with it first-class cricket. The club was founded about 1750 and in its heyday 20 or 30 years later defeated All-England 29 times in ten years, the most famous occasion being in 1777 when it won by an innings and 168 runs. This was the match in which Aylward, who is buried in Corhampton churchyard, scored 167 not out, batting from five o'clock on a Wednesday until three o'clock on the following Friday. Not all the leading members of the club, however, came from Hambledon itself. Thomas Brett, who opened the innings with Lord Tankerville in the great 1777 match (though they scored only a dozen between them) and who was reputed 'the fastest and straightest bowler that ever was known', was born in Catherington a few miles away, and several others came from over the Surrey border. Broadhalfpenny Down, where the club played, and the Bat and Ball Inn on top of it which was their headquarters, lie a good two miles further on from the village and command a huge view of a landscape almost as unspoilt now as it was then; though the architecture of the inn does not match its historical interest. The mainspring and historian of the club was Richard Nyren, the son of the landlord of the inn in its greatest days and himself no mean performer (he made 37 in the 1777 match). His *Cricketer's Guide and Recollections* gives the best existing account of early cricket and cricketers.

In its heyday the club held much the same position in the cricket world as that held to-day by the M.C.C., whose foundation in 1787 was largely due to the initiative of the club's then president, and the rules it passed were universally observed.

Hambledon itself lies in a shallow valley of the chalkland foothills. It was a market town in the Middle Ages, but by the eighteenth century it had shrunk to the status of a large village. Its church is almost a textbook of medieval ecclesiastical architecture, and on the slope of the ridge on which it stands there is one of the few important wine-growing vineyards in England, the property of Major-General Sir Guy Salisbury-Jones.

A short distance down the Meon valley from Droxford, but on the east bank of the river, is Soberton. This widespread village has an old though small core around its church, a straggling main street a little south of it, and further afield some Victorian cottages scattered over former heathland. The church itself is architecturally rather puzzling, but its finest part is the south transept, on the jambs of whose two lancet east windows are the remains of some very impressive wall-paintings. Nearly all traces of colouring have disappeared, but the black outline of parts of the designs remains clear. They depict Saints Anne, Catherine and Margaret, with a fourth unidentified but doubtless saintly female, and have been attributed to about 1300. The transept as a whole has a Georgian atmosphere, with box pews. In the village Admiral Anson, another of the great sea-commanders of the eighteenth century, lived for some time, and when rewarded for a victory over the French in 1747 he took the title of Baron Anson of Soberton.

Soon after Soberton the country changes, becoming flatter and more thickly timbered as the chalk is left behind and the Meon flows on through the claylands nearer the seaboard. At Wickham, where the road from Portsmouth to Winchester crosses the river, the main road that has hitherto followed the valley leaves it and strikes away for Fareham. Wickham, which is perhaps Hampshire's finest village, is built round a great rectangular 'square' that was probably laid out to accommodate the fair the village has possessed since 1268, with an island block of buildings at its northern end and some charming Georgian houses on either side. In the narrow and homely Bridge Street that leads eastwards from the square is Chesapeake Mill, so called because when it was built in 1820 its internal woodwork was taken from the American frigate *Chesapeake,* defeated and captured by the British *Shannon* in the most famous single-ship action of the unhappy war of 1812-14 between the two peoples. As its name suggests, the village was the birthplace of Bishop William of Wykeham.

Fareham stands midway between Southampton and Portsmouth at the head of a creek of Portsmouth Harbour that is really the estuary of the little Wallington river, which though only a few miles long has the local characteristic of widening greatly as it nears the sea. From the Middle Ages to Victorian times it was a market town and small port, to which until the 1850s ships of 300 tons could still come to exchange coal and timber for the bricks called 'Fareham Reds' and the tiles and pottery that it manufactured. In Georgian days, too, senior naval officers had a *penchant* for retiring to it. To-day it is expanding fast, but its centre of gravity has moved from the old north-south High Street to an east-west thoroughfare that was part of the Southampton-Portsmouth main road until a bypass was built south of the town to circumvent the bottleneck that it was becoming. The High Street has thus become something of a commercial backwater, largely unspoilt although many of its fine Georgian houses have been converted to business or professional purposes and the volume of traffic through it has inevitably grown of late. Professor Pevsner has described it as 'one of the best country-town streets in the south of England'.

At Funtley, a mile and a half north-east of Fareham, the ironmaster Henry Cort who invented the reverberatory furnace and the rolling mill in the 1780s built the first iron mill. The remains of the two millraces and the dry millpond can still be seen beside the Meon, and the ironmaster's house nearby still stands, though with a good deal of modern addition and alteration. There are no ironworks there now, though the brickworks that have made 'Fareham Reds' for nearly three centuries are still functioning.

A couple of miles west of Fareham and on the left of the Southampton road is Titchfield on the Meon, which in spite of being nearly three miles from the river's mouth was also a small port in the Middle Ages, with an abbey founded in the thirteenth century. After Henry VIII's dissolution of the monasteries the abbey, which stands half-a-mile on the other side of the main road to Southampton, was given to his minister Thomas Wriothesley, Earl of Southampton, for services rendered, notably in helping the King to get rid of his first wife Catherine of Aragon. Wriothesley, whose accumulations in Hampshire alone also included the lands and revenues of Hyde and Beaulieu Abbeys, converted parts of the building into a mansion called Place House. Here his family, including his grandson the third earl who was Shakespeare's friend and patron, lived for several generations, but in the seventeenth century the house passed out of their possession. In the eighteenth it ceased to be lived in and it was largely demolished in 1781, though substantial parts of the gatehouse and of its flanking wings that had been fashioned out of the Abbey nave still remain, a splendid ruin overlooking a fishpond guarded by an ancient oak. Titchfield itself ceased to be a port of any importance after the estuary of the Meon was drained in the seventeenth century, though its buildings suggest that it must still have had some modest prosperity in the eighteenth. The architecture of its wide streets is predominantly of Georgian brick, though with much evidence, especially behind the façades, of timber-frame construction – very pleasing as an *ensemble*, though there are few large houses to compare with Fareham's best. In the south chapel of the church, which also has a fine Norman west doorway and on the west wall a modern mural of the Miraculous Draught of Fishes, there is the magnificent tomb of several of the Southampton family.

Titchfield Haven, where the Meon flows into the Solent, is rather attractive, but the same cannot be said of Lee-on-the-Solent two miles east along the coast towards Gosport. This is a small seaside resort which began to grow in the late nineteenth century but whose pier has long since vanished and the branch railway to which has also long been closed. Its chief surviving asset is its view across to the Isle of Wight.

FIVE

Portsmouth and its Environs

Portsmouth and Southampton, though only a few miles apart with overlapping hinterlands, are surprisingly independent of each other, or would seem so unless one bears in mind that while one is our greatest naval base the other is one of our greatest merchant ports. They have one common characteristic, however, for each has experienced a remarkable post-war renaissance and development; though slower off the mark in Portsmouth's case, since it was left to face even greater handicaps.

Nevertheless Portsmouth is now living through what is perhaps the period of greatest change in all its long history, for it is breaking out of the mould which that history imposed on it; indeed one could almost say out of the trap in which geography and history had combined to place it. For a long time geography had served it well. Geographical factors made it a great naval base, since although its harbour, the second splendid natural haven of the Hampshire coast, has no inflowing river like Southampton's two, but lies shut in and protected on the landward side by the long chalk outlier called Portsdown Hill, this has meant that together with the Spithead anchorage at its mouth and under the lee of the Isle of Wight it became a snug and secure place for a great fleet and its appurtenances, supplies and dockyard.

Portsmouth therefore grew around the dockyard upon which and on other defence and allied establishments two out of every five of its menfolk are still dependent for employment. But the dockyard was not only the great *raison d'être* of its growth but paradoxically it also became the first of the two disadvantages from which it has suffered in modern times and is only now breaking free. For the development of the dockyard has meant that Portsmouth has been a town with all its eggs in one basket. Until very recently it had relatively little other industry or trade and therefore was so hard hit by the modern shrinkage of the navy that it was talked of as a dying city; a gloomy forecast which it is now disproving. This then has been the handicap imposed by its history; but the other difficulty from which it is striving to escape has been imposed by geography. It grew up on an island – indeed it is the only British city on an island site – linked to the mainland merely by a single road-bridge across the narrow Port Creek, until the railway bridge appeared in the nineteenth century, followed by a second road-bridge well on in the twentieth. When therefore it had expanded to cover practically the whole of its island by about 1900 it found itself hampered in its further growth by problems of transport and communication. But the solutions to its two difficulties are bound up closely together. In the last twenty years Portsmouth has set to work with a will to attract new and varied industries. To find land for these and to house the workers in them it has had to turn largely to the mainland. Only thus can it have the future it seeks. But that means an escalation of its traffic and transport problems with which it is now grappling.

The first 'Old Portsmouth', however, was not on Portsea Island at all, but on a tongue of land jutting out into the northern end of the harbour, where at Portchester a great Roman fort arose in the third century A.D. as one of the strongholds built to defend the south and east coasts of the province of Britain against Saxon pirates. Its entire defensive wall, ten feet thick and originally 20 or more in height, still survives; indeed it is the only Roman fortress in northern Europe whose *enceinte* stands intact to-day; as do 14 of its original projecting D-shaped bastions (a notable feature of late third-century Roman military architecture) on which the giant catapults called *ballistae* could be mounted to provide both forward and flanking fire. Recent excavations conducted by the distinguished Portsmouth-born archaeologist Professor Cunliffe have shown that the military occupation of the fort ended about 370, a generation or more before the close of Roman rule in Britain; perhaps, he suggests, through the substitution of Clausentum on the Itchen as a coastal fortress. They have also proved, however, that it was occupied again very early in Saxon days and continued to be inhabited sporadically until the Norman period. Then in the twelfth century it was transformed into a medieval castle by the building of a keep and the walling-off of a small inner bailey with a moat at the north-west corner of the Roman enclosure, the rest of which became the outer bailey. Within the latter an Augustinian priory was founded at about the same time, whose chapel with its splendid western front and delightful mouldings still stands, though the monks soon moved away to a new priory at Southwick on the other side of Portsdown Hill, perhaps because the near neighbourhood of a garrison of rough and no doubt licentious men-at-arms was too much for them. Portchester castle was important for about a hundred years both as a strongpoint for Plantagenet monarchs entering or leaving the country and a base for their hunting-parties in the neighbouring Forest of Bere. Then for a time it was neglected, but it came into favour again as a royal residence after a series of alterations and improvements in the fourteenth century. Neglected again after another hundred years, it was eventually sold by the Crown in 1632, though its private owners afterwards leased it occasionally to house prisoners-of-war, mostly Frenchmen some of whose names can still be seen carved or scratched on the walls. In 1926 it was transferred by its last owner to what is now the Ministry of Public Building and Works, and is visited yearly by thousands of people.

To the landward of the castle a rabidly suburban rash of buildings has spread thickly over the coastal strip at the foot of Portsdown Hill, but in its immediate neighbourhood there remains a surprisingly unspoilt and wholly delightful village centre whose mainly eighteenth-century houses make a modest foil to the great keep.

Portsmouth proper was brought into existence by the Norman Conquest, though not immediately. Since for a century and a half afterwards both sides of the Channel were under a common rule, their rulers in their travels between them sometimes sailed from or landed at this harbour that was so conveniently opposite the mouth of the river Seine which formed the axis of their duchy of Normandy. At first they came and went from Portchester, but when the northern part of the harbour apparently began to silt up and make it difficult to reach the castle by water a flourishing little town grew up in the twelfth century on the east side of the harbour mouth around a small inlet called the Camber. About 1180 a wealthy local merchant and shipowner founded a chapel there dedicated to the recently martyred Archbishop Thomas à Becket of Canterbury, parts of which, though greatly altered and enlarged, survive to-day in what was formerly the parish church of St Thomas and is now Portsmouth Cathedral.

In 1194 King Richard the Lion-Heart, engaged in raising money for a war with France by the sale of charters of privileges to towns among other means, granted one to Portsmouth and thus established the town as a municipal entity; and about 1212 a second religious establishment was founded, the Domus Dei, which like that at Southampton was an almshouse and hospice for travellers. After performing these functions for over 300 years it was dissolved by Henry VIII along with other religious houses at the Reformation, the buildings becoming first a magazine and then the residence of the military governor, after which they fell into disrepair until little survived but the chapel, which was restored in 1867-8 to become the garrison church. Blitzed in the Second World War, it is now a roofless ruin standing near the Grand Parade at the foot of the High Street.

After Richard's brother and successor John allowed the bulk of the French provinces to slip from his hands the fortunes of the town seem to have flagged. It had some trade and was from time to time the mustering-place of fleets and armies for the wars with France. Nevertheless in both respects it was less important than Southampton, of which it was legally only an outport. But it seems likely that before the end of the fourteenth century it was enclosed within a simple earthwork and moat, and early in the fifteenth its first stone defensive work, the Round Tower, was built at the mouth of the harbour. In any case its natural defences were good. On the north side of the town a creek ran in from the harbour close to the present side of the torpedo and anti-submarine establishment H.M.S. *Vernon* to approximately where Guildhall Square now is. After being dammed up to provide the headwaters for a mill, this covered the town on this site by an extensive pond or lake called the Mill Pond; while to the south-east it was covered by a marsh called the Little Morass near the present Pier Road.

In the Tudor period Portsmouth's possibilities as a naval base began to be realised. Henry VII built a dry dock about half-a-mile up-harbour from the town and a Square Tower at the seaward end of the High Street, a little further towards the sea than the Round Tower and therefore just outside the harbour mouth. Henry VIII, who was genuinely interested in naval matters and determined to keep abreast of or outrival France, which had lately fortified Le Havre at the mouth of the Seine, strengthened the town's defences and built a fort afterwards called Southsea Castle on the shore about a mile east of the Round Tower. In his reign and Elizabeth I's, however, other dockyards arose at Woolwich, Deptford and Chatham on the Thames and Medway which for a time eclipsed Portsmouth's because of their greater proximity to London and accessibility to the sources of supply of timber and other naval stores. Nevertheless under Elizabeth the defences were strengthened further and all hedges, buildings and other obstacles to a clear field of fire within 50 yards of the ramparts were removed. It was the maintenance for centuries of these ramparts and the continued insistence on this unobstructed field of fire which gave Portsmouth its peculiar urban pattern of several separate areas, since both it and its later satellite Portsea grew up within constricting fortifications with a belt of unbuilt-on land around each of them, and before these fortifications were demolished their eighteenth- and nineteenth-century suburbs had developed apart from the parent towns.

Although Charles I spent more money on the navy and the defences of Portsmouth than is usually realised, it was during the Commonwealth period which followed the Civil War and his execution that the second and more lasting rise of Portsmouth as a dockyard and naval base began. Under Charles II a Flemish engineer, Sir Bernard de Gomme, completely rebuilt the towns's fortifications on the principles of which his contemporary the Frenchman Vauban was the greatest exponent. The expulsion of Charles's brother and successor James II by the Bloodless Revolution of 1688 and the war with France which followed his flight to that country then brought about a revolution in English foreign policy which was of vital importance to Portsmouth. For the previous hundred years, during which England's main enemies had been the Spaniards as rulers of the Netherlands which so closely threatened the Thames and after them the Dutch, Chatham's geographical position had made it the country's main naval base; but now that France had again become the foe the same dictates of geography rapidly brought Portsmouth – facing France as it did – to the premier place by the end of the seventeenth century.

The whole town had hitherto lain within the narrow limits of its fortifications, but as the dockyard and its labour force grew during the eighteenth-century wars against France a virtually separate township developed to the north on what was then known as the Common. This satellite town was populated chiefly by dockyard workers and keepers of taverns, shops and brothels that catered for the navy. It afterwards took the name of Portsea and was enclosed by ramparts of its own in the 1770s. Towards the end of the century the same process of overspill began to repeat itself and yet another township grew up in its turn outside these newer walls. This lay mainly along the line of the present Commercial Road and was called Landport after the principal landward gate of the old town. It was largely working-class in character. Then in the early decades of the nineteenth century a fourth town began to take shape on Southsea Common, as the wasteland behind Southsea Castle had come to be called after the building of that fort. Large parts of this area had hitherto consisted of ill-drained marshes such as the Little Morass, but a section had been sold to the Government in 1785 when additional land near the Castle was needed for military purposes. This had the effect of preventing Victorian speculators from building up to and along the shore after the Common had been drained, and thus has created a substantial strip of land free from buildings between the sea and the built-up part of Southsea, which, though beginning as a residential suburb, developed into a holiday resort during the nineteenth century. In 1923 the Corporation bought this still unbuilt-on shoreward strip of the Common from the War Department (from which they had rented the use of it for some time previously) and converted some of it into pleasure-gardens that enhanced the attractions of the flourishing seaside resort which Southsea had by then become.

Elsewhere, growth had also been prodigious in the nineteenth century. Landport succeeded Old Portsmouth as the town's centre of gravity, a change which was marked by the building in 1886-90 of a magnificent new guildhall there to replace a much smaller predecessor in the High Street of the old town; and that part of Landport Road (later significantly renamed Commercial Road) which lay north of the railway developed into an important shopping centre. Buildings spread northward and eastward over the island, linking up and absorbing the former villages and hamlets of Kingston, Fratton, Copnor, Milton, Tipner and Hilsea. The built-up area of the borough nearly doubled in the last quarter of the century, and early in the twentieth it began to sprawl on to the mainland, swamping the old bridgehead village of Cosham. Subsequently it has spread for miles along the roads towards London, Southampton and Chichester, while still leaving some unspoilt stretches or pockets of country at the sides of these roads.

In the 1870s and 1880s the now redundant ramparts of Portsmouth and Portsea were demolished, except that the seaward line of Portsmouth's walls from the King's Bastion at the south-east corner to the Square Tower was retained as still providing important sites for guns covering the immediate approaches to the harbour, and was used as part of the town's defences up to and throughout the Second World War. The sites of the vanished ramparts and of the Mill Pond which was filled in at the same time were used for barracks, the United Services Recreation Grounds, a public park named after Queen Victoria and further extensions of the dockyard.

At practically the same time as the old fortifications were coming down, however, new ones were being built further afield. An exaggerated fear of French invasion during the reign of the Emperor Napoleon III prompted Britain's prime minister Lord Palmerston to sanction a scheme, implemented during the 1860s and 1870s, for the building of a line of forts on the crest of Portsdown Hill, facing landwards to meet any attack from a force which might have landed further along the coast, as well as another line across the Gosport peninsula on the far side of the harbour, and three (to which a smaller fourth off St Helens was presently added) on the Solent shoals for the protection of Spithead. These forts constituted the last ring fortifications to be built around any European city in the nineteenth century and made Portsmouth for a time one of the most strongly defended places in the world; but they became rather unjustly known locally as 'Palmerston's Folly' in the reaction which followed the panic. After the Second World War the Portsdown forts met diverse fates. Fort Southwick became an extensive radar establishment; Forts Widley and Purbrook have been taken over by the Corporation and the former thrown open to the public while the latter is being worked on for the same purpose; Forts Nelson and Farlington became derelict; and Fort Wallington was bought for use as a storage depot and partly demolished. Of the forts beyond Gosport one has been pulled down, one is being restored as an ancient monument, and three are still in Service occupation. The Solent forts, which had been manned during that war, still belong to the Ministry of Defence, which considered selling them until the City Council, alerted by some of the suggestions for their use which were immediately bandied about as to the possibility of their being plastered with enormous advertisements and the like, and intervened to secure the dropping of the idea for the time being.

During the Second World War the city suffered terribly from 67 bombing raids. The main shopping centres were almost obliterated; 7000 homes were destroyed; the Guildhall was burnt out (though it was afterwards restored); the fine High Street that had been one of the prides of the old town was half ruined; churches, schools, hospitals, theatres and cinemas were wiped out; and the population was reduced by evacuation (besides a thousand killed) from 260,000 to an estimated 143,000 at the worst moment of the blitz. After the war people began to come back and the population soon rose again to the quarter-million mark. Portsmouth was now faced by a problem of reconstruction, complicated by the run-down of the navy. The most pressing aspect of the problem was to provide housing quickly, but since it was desirable to rebuild at a lower density than before and there was a shortage of land within the city boundaries, accommodation had to be provided outside them for at least 40,000 people. (The population of the city in 1975 was about 220,000.) Fortunately the Corporation had been foresighted and courageous enough to buy before the war ended nearly 2000 acres of land at Leigh Park near Havant. Here a satellite town with its own industrial estate and a layout of an outmoded and rather dreary garden-city type has arisen to take the greater part of the overspill. In the subsequent years other great housing estates have been built within the city limits, both on the mainland at Farlington and on the slopes of Portsdown Hill, as well as on Portsea Island itself. Here there has not only been rebuilding on blitzed areas but thousands of poor houses have been cleared away to make possible the residential redevelopment of the districts concerned. Probably the most striking example of this is the Somerstown region of east Southsea, where towering blocks of flats have sprung up like a miniature Manhattan to replace the former terrace-houses. However startling and to some people aesthetically unwelcome these blocks and perhaps still more those on the Portsdown slopes may be, this solution of the problem of finding space by building high has brought sunlight and open air into these neighbourhoods.

But there was another and in the long run even greater difficulty facing a city so dependent on one main industry, and that one so closely linked with the defence services as the dockyard was. This was the renewed reduction of the navy which followed the Second World War, even greater than that after the First. That first reduction in the 1920s and 1930s had been met by the booming of Southsea as a holiday resort, but during and after the blitz it had of course completely ceased to function as such; and though it soon recovered its popularity it could not by itself, in view of the huge capital expenditure facing the city, have the same steadying influence on its economy as before. For the moment Portsmouth seemed to have been overtaken and overwhelmed by the march of events. A long slow decline as a city living on its memories might have lain before it.

But now the near-miracle began; not merely a resurgence but a transformation. Reaching out for a new vitality, the historic seaport has set itself to attract as many and varied light industries as possible. On the development and prosperity of these and on the expansion of the commerce of the Camber it is basing its hopes for the future. An advantage of this policy is that whereas the general level of dockyard wages has been low (though there has been some improvement in them and no doubt will be more in the future) the introduction of these private light manufacturing industries will offer higher wage-rates as well as more stable employment, and also more opportunities of work.

For these new industries land again was needed, and as with the rehousing problem recourse had largely to be made to the mainland. The Council made land available at Farlington, where an industrial estate has sprung up, as well as in several districts of Portsea Island. The steady build-up of industry and commerce that has followed has perhaps been Portsmouth's greatest post-war achievement. To quote a *Financial Times* survey, 'the city has become one of the largest centres of employment in south-east England outside London'.

To meet the need for industrial land and also to provide more public open spaces and playing-fields, land has been and is being reclaimed from the sea, both in the shallow Langstone Harbour on the east side of the island and in the north of Portsmouth Harbour itself where two chalk bunds have been built, the area enclosed by which is being rapidly transformed into land that will be used mainly to provide a marina for a

13 Opposite *The river Test, most famous for fishing of all the chalk streams of southern England, near Stockbridge.*

thousand craft, industrial sites, and facilities for recreation. Land and buildings released by the Ministry of Defence have also been adapted to residential, recreational, cultural and public amenity purposes. In 1958-60 the Council bought Southsea Castle, the Round and Square Towers and the surviving stretch of the walls that had so long guarded the approach to the harbour mouth, restored them, laid out public walks along the line of the ramparts and converted the Castle into a museum depicting the naval and military history of the town. After the Portsmouth garrison was closed in 1960, too, the former Clarence Barracks in Alexandra Road were made into a city museum and art gallery. Fort Cumberland, built in the middle of the eighteenth century at the eastern end of Portsea Island's beach in order to guard the narrow entrance into Langstone Harbour and named after George II's son the 'Butcher' victor of Culloden, is also no longer in military use but under the control of the Department of the Environment's Directorate of Ancient Monuments.

Perhaps the most striking change of all is the new city centre which is being created in the area around the restored Guildhall. The previous centre which has been situated there for the greater part of a century dated not only from the great days of British naval expansion but equally from the worst days of British town-planning. The awkward siting of the Guildhall, jammed up against the railway which bisected the centre from east to west, and the inability of the lower end of Commercial Road with its scattering of small shops, banks, office buildings and public-houses to provide it with a decent setting were characteristic of the period. After a plan prepared by Lord Esher as co-ordinating architect had received the approval of a public enquiry the demolition of most of these old buildings has cleared the way for a new and extensive traffic-free Guildhall Square where additional civic offices, enlarged premises for the city's Polytechnic, a new central library and modern office-blocks and shops have arisen or are now arising.

But problems still remain. 40 per cent of Portsmouth men are still dependent on the defence services in one way or another for their employment. The level of unemployment, though below the national average, is usually not far short of double that for London and the south-east, and the abler and more ambitious of the younger folk still tend to drift away, while many of those who remain to work in the city go to

14 Opposite *Norman work in Romsey Abbey, the finest church in Hampshire and perhaps in all the south of England.*

live on the municipal estates outside it or on the verge of its boundaries when they marry. Nor is it only the young who move outwards. A survey in 1965 showed that out of 83,000 people whose work was on Portsea Island 31,000 travelled from the mainland, 21,000 of them from outside the city limits and three-quarters of them by car or bus, which in view of the restricted road access to the island meant wearisome journeys and long traffic jams at every rush hour. Although a second road connection between the island and the mainland (besides the original one over Portsbridge) had been made in 1941 by the Eastern Road, leaving the mainland's east-west coast road at Drayton and running close to Langstone Harbour after crossing the eastern end of Port Creek, by the 1960s Portsmouth's road system had become more inadequate than ever even with this reinforcement. In 1965 the City Council therefore adopted a plan for a new road pattern providing for two north-south routes, on the east and west sides of the island respectively, linked together at the southern end by an east-west road; the whole to form a U-shaped loop crossed at its top by the new south coast trunk road M27. An enlarged and extended Eastern Road, that is, will form a link from the M27 to the new east-west road in the south of the island which is already under construction; while on the west side of the city another north-south road will similarly leave the M27, cross the reclaimed land in the north of the harbour and travel along the island's western shore before veering into the city. The plan also included an inner ring road which has already been built, by-passing the Commercial Road shopping and business area north of the Guildhall and enabling this to be closed to traffic and a pedestrian shopping precinct to be created.

Meanwhile Old Portsmouth, which by the middle of the nineteenth century had become something of a backwater, has now been transformed into a fashionable residential quarter. Many of the old houses which survived the savage bombing have been discreetly restored, retaining in a number of cases their demure eighteenth-century character with shallow segmental windows on the first floor; and new flats (though most of them are unfortunately of a low architectural standard) have arisen on the bombed sites. In the background, however, looms the power-station, the biggest building in Portsmouth, lumpy and obtrusive. The High Street starts well with the Grammar School on the left from the landward end and Buckingham House, where Charles I's favourite the Duke of

Buckingham was murdered, a little further along; but the rebuilt middle stretch of that side is now a wretched jumble of nondescript buildings. On the right, however, Lombard Street leads past the east end of the cathedral to the pleasantest group of old houses surviving in the old town. The cathedral itself was for 600 years the parish church of St Thomas until Portsmouth became a diocese in 1927, but the enlargements made afterwards to provide for its new role have deprived it of much of its character as a medium-sized town church without making it in size or splendour anything like the traditional idea of a cathedral. To be fair, however, the problem was difficult. Eastward expansion was impossible because of the excellent medieval work at that end; large-scale lateral expansion would have produced a weirdly-shaped building; westward expansion would have been comparatively easy if the tower had been demolished, but it was a familiar landmark in the city then, before the power-station and other tall buildings had arisen comparatively close at hand. The solution had therefore to be westward expansion while retaining the tower.

At the seaward end of High Street stands the Square Tower with a bust of Charles I on the wall facing the street, which he presented to the town in 1635 in acknowledgement of the inhabitants' rejoicing in common with all good Protestants when, while Prince of Wales, he returned from a visit to Spain to court a Catholic princess without having won her hand. The inscription originally closed with the sentence – 'There was the greatest applause for his safety throughout the kingdom that ever was known or heard of' – but during the Civil War, when the town had been captured by the Parliamentarians after a short siege, this sentence was erased by the victors.

Where the High Street turns right and becomes Broad Street a peninsula between the harbour mouth and the Camber begins which is called Point. This had originally been left outside the town's defences with a wall built across its neck, pierced in James II's reign by King James's Gate, as a nearby tablet records.* But during the seventeenth century many houses arose on the little peninsula, which came to be regarded as not only physically outside the town but also to a great extent outside its law. Among the many privileges it enjoyed which were denied

---

* This wall and gate were removed shortly after 1860.

to residents within the town was the right of licensed victuallers to keep their houses open both day and night. Hence, with 41 beerhouses, brandy-shops, brothels and sleezy coffee-houses in 1716, it won an evil reputation for drunkenness, brawls and immorality, and was sometimes said (though doubtless with some exaggeration) to be the wickedest place in Europe.

On the left at the foot of the High Street is Grand Parade, a wide square formerly used as a military parade-ground before and after services at the neighbouring Garrison Church, with a rather engaging row of houses on its north-west side – though the same cannot be said of the rebuilt ones opposite to them. The square is open at its far end to the backs of the surviving ramparts, and one can (and should) mount to the old Saluting Platform to survey the views both towards the Isle of Wight and up-harbour, and then walk in this latter direction to the Square Tower, afterwards descending and strolling through the still picturesque little residential area between Broad Street and the water. Here the name of Semaphore House recalls the time when, by means of a chain of giant wooden semaphores, the first of which straddled the roof of the Square Tower and the rest stood on hills within sight of each other by telescope until the last was reached on the Admiralty roof, a message could be sent or received in ten minutes. The last message to be sent by this method was taken down in Portsmouth on 31 December 1847. A little further along and on the water's edge is the charming weatherboarded Quebec House, built in 1754 as a bathing-house and later taken over and given its name by the Quebec Hotel next door, which was so called because it had become a rendezvous for passengers to and from North America. On the extremity of Point which one soon reaches, and from which there is a fine view up-harbour and of the dockyard on the right, there are three survivors of its former taverns, all basically Georgian and one of them commemorating by the names of its bars the circumnavigation exploit of the Portsmuthian Sir Alec Rose in his little yacht *The Lively Lady*.

By passing round Vosper Thorneycroft's shipbuilding and engineering yard in White Hart Road, and then rounding the *Vernon* torpedo-training school, the dockyard may be reached. The final approach to it is along the Hard, lined with hostelries bearing names redolent of eighteenth-century naval glories, such as the Ship Anson and the Keppel's Head – in addition to a tattooist's establishment whose proprietor has prudently posted a notice proclaiming that he does not tattoo girls. Passing through the Main Gate in a surviving stretch of the original dockyard wall built in Queen Anne's reign, one may walk up past boathouses and red-brick stores dating from the eighteenth century to visit H.M.S. *Victory* lying permanently in dry dock and the *Victory* Museum opposite her. The eighteenth-century dockyard church may also be visited, but most of the rest of the yard is not generally accessible to the public.

Outside the dockyard gates and wall, and partly between them and Old Portsmouth, lies Portsea. Already rather decayed before the Second World War, it suffered heavy bombing in this and was afterwards partly rebuilt in a piecemeal way; though in Charlotte Street a complex of shops, offices and much else has been developed which makes a pleasant composition.

Gosport on the opposite or western side of Portsmouth Harbour was not a place of any size or importance until the seventeenth century, when it grew into a small town and began to be enclosed within defensive ramparts. These fortifications were completed in the eighteenth century and were never systematically demolished as those of Portsmouth were, so that large parts of them survived well into the twentieth century. To-day, however, only two fragments remain; a long but relatively inaccessible stretch in the grounds of St George's Barracks near Weevil Lane*, where most of the rampart survives and the moat, though nearly all filled in, can easily be distinguished; and a bastion on the south side of Holy Trinity Church, outside which a section of the moat can still be seen, though nearly empty at high tide.

After about 1830 the town began to sprawl beyond its walls, though this expansion was presently checked by the construction of the line of five forts from Elson on Portsmouth Harbour to Gomer on the coast of the Solent which formed part of Palmerston's mid-Victorian defence scheme. An outer line of three more, running across the Gosport peninsula

---

* Weevil Lane presumably owes its name to the presence in it of the Royal Clarence Victualling Yard, established in 1828 and named after the Duke of Clarence (afterwards William IV), who had become Lord High Admiral in the previous year. The presence of weevils in navy biscuits had long been notorious. Indeed, it was a saying among seamen that if when a piece of biscuit was rapped on the deck weevils tumbled out it was a good one; a bad biscuit, which even weevils would not touch, merely crumbled. The Yard and the lane in which it stood would be sardonically said to be swarming with these insects.

from Lee-on-the-Solent to Fareham, was also proposed, but of these only Fort Fareham (now transformed into an industrial site) was ever built. After the Second World War Gosport's development stretched far afield and it is now a spread-out town, pleasantly leafy in its better parts though less attractive in others. Its comparatively wide and curving High Street is still moderately pleasing; and its former waterfront, which lacked charm, has been replaced by a new promenade to the south of the landing-place of the ferry from Portsmouth. From this promenade a striking panorama of the remains of the latter's old fortifications and of the dockyard can be seen; and between it and the parish church of Holy Trinity an ambitious new housing scheme has been developed, whose chief features are four tower-blocks of flats, two of 16 storeys and two of 11, which are regarded with mixed feelings by some of the inhabitants of Gosport. The church, built in 1696, contains the celebrated 'Handel Organ' which was originally at Canons Park, Stanmore, where the great musician was organist to the Duke of Chandos, and was brought to Gosport in the middle of the eighteenth century. In 1887-89 the church was completely restored by Blomfield, who turned the old plain building into a rather crude version of a Lombard basilica and added a campanile which became a notable landmark of the town and still, though overtopped by the new flats, refuses to be overwhelmed by them.

Across Haslar Creek, which runs in from the Harbour to the south of the town proper, are the residential suburb of Alverstoke and the Haslar Royal Naval Hospital, which was built in the middle of the eighteenth century and whose buildings are of dun brick in rather austere Georgian style. The original village of Alverstoke was dominated by its church, around which its core still clusters, with narrow streets leading into a tiny and roughly triangular 'square'. Now, however, the former village has spread in every direction; sometimes rather insensitively, though it has an architectural *tour-de-force* in the shape of the Crescent. Begun in 1826, this was meant to be the centrepiece of a new marine town which was to have been called Anglesea after its promoter, the Marquess of Anglesey who was Wellington's brother-in-law and commanded the cavalry at Waterloo. Nothing much else of this projected town, however, was built until the blank spaces were filled in much later with ordinary suburban development. As a piece of grand urban planning of the early nineteenth century the Crescent has been pronounced unsurpassed in Hampshire.

On the eastern side of Portsmouth is Bedhampton, a growing residential area with an oasis of substantial old houses in the village centre lying south of the main road to Havant. At one of these, Lower Mill House, Keats stayed for a time while he was writing *The Eve of St Agnes*; but the gem is The Elms, dating possibly from the seventeenth century or even earlier, gothicized in the eighteenth and much altered and enlarged in the nineteenth. The manor-house is mainly nineteenth-century but has some older work in the centre. The church has a Norman arch but has been too much gone over in Victorian times to be really attractive.

Havant, until well on in the nineteenth century, was a small market-town with its own little port a mile away at Langstone on the creek which links the harbour of that name to Chichester Harbour and separates Hayling Island from the mainland. Its original layout was a simple cross of four cardinal streets centring on St Faith's church, which is in part medieval but much restored and in part Victorian. In East and South Streets there are some pleasant Georgian houses, but owing to a devastating fire in 1760 there is only one half-timbered building remaining, 'The Old House at Home' in South Street. In the twentieth century residential fringes developed round the little town and after the Second World War an industrial estate arose to the north which connected it to Portsmouth's overspill town of Leigh Park, making it first a large satellite of the city and latterly a borough in its own right. As such it embraces not only Bedhampton but also Purbrook, Waterlooville and Cowplain on the Portsmouth-London road, Leigh Park, Warblington and Emsworth to the eastward, and Hayling Island, making a total population of over 110,000.

Langstone, to-day a well-known sailing centre, has a row of picturesque cottages facing the village street and on the frontage to the harbour a comfortable inn and an old mill now converted into a most attractive house. The harbour is an overwintering area for dark-breasted brent geese, which migrate to this country from Siberia in the late autumn. From the village a path runs along the shore to Warblington and Emsworth. The former, once the most important place in its own parish, became a deserted village when Emsworth obtained the right to a market and a yearly fair in the thirteenth century and so eclipsed it in importance. Now, though a small residential district has developed on the main Havant-Emsworth road, the site of the old village half-a-mile to seaward is an area of undisturbed farmland stretching around a church, some farm buildings and a fragment of a castle. The church has a tower whose lowest stage was reconstructed in the thirteenth century but whose second stage is Saxon with archways of Roman tiles, and a fourteenth-century wooden porch probably built from ships' timbers. Most of the rest of the building is late twelfth-century and early thirteenth; and in the churchyard are a massive yew whose trunk is 18 feet in circumference and several interesting gravestones. The castle was a moated and fortified manor-house built on the site of an earlier fortified building by Margaret Countess of Salisbury in the early part of the reign of Henry VIII (in the later part of which he had her executed for what in effect was the crime of belonging to a family of potentially rival royal blood). It was ruined in the Civil War, leaving only an octagonal turret of the gatehouse and a few other fragments.

Nearly all of Emsworth is just inside the county boundary formed here by the little river Ems and its broad estuary, though some of the tiny town spills over into Sussex by virtue of being on the other side of the river. It was once a minor fishing and trading port at the head of a channel of Chichester Harbour into which the Ems flows, and indeed in the sixteenth century most of the trade of the 'port of Chichester' passed through it. In the eighteenth it became particularly prosperous, and though it was never very large there are some lovely old houses hidden away in Tower Street, Queen Street and South Street. But in the nineteenth century it declined; and at the beginning of the twentieth its principal occupation, the production of oysters (which local patriotism claimed excelled even the 'natives' of Whitstable and Colchester in size and flavour) suffered a fatal blow when several of the guests at a civic banquet in Winchester, including the dean of the cathedral, were fatally smitten by typhoid fever after eating some of them. It was asserted that they had been polluted by the effluent discharged into the town harbour through a recently-built sewer, and though nothing was proved the sale of Emsworth oysters was banned in London and collapsed elsewhere. Some of the old oyster-smacks still lie rotting where they were abandoned in the harbour, on whose shores two of the tide-mills which gristed the locally-grown corn still stand and serve as storehouses.

On the other hand smuggling, which from remote antiquity had been a main occupation of the local maritime community, continued to flourish to such an extent that, according to a reliable and scholarly septuagenarian resident, the police did not dare to patrol South Street, leading down to the harbour, except in pairs. Apart from this semi-clandestine activity, however, the town developed an atmosphere of staid decay which it wore until a few years ago; but now it has become a fashionable minor yachting centre with boat-building yards and rope-, net- and sail-works, while antique shops and cosy little restaurants vie with the taverns of South Street. With the growth of traffic along the main south-coast road (A27) which passes through the town its centre became more and more of a bottleneck until in 1974 a bypass was made to avoid it.

Hayling Island until the present century was merely an expanse of flat fields, substantial farmsteads and straggling and rather formless hamlets. Much of its north and centre is still like that, but with two markedly differing exceptions. St Paul's church at North Hayling is a fine example of a typical village church of the Norman and Early English periods, while the other exception is the holiday camps near the shore on the western side. In the village of South Hayling there is another impressive church, dating from the thirteenth century; but the southern seaboard of the island only began to be developed after the building of the first bridge from Havant and Langstone in 1822-4. A hotel, part of a crescent, and two or three villas were built — prematurely, as it proved, for over-sanguine expectations were disappointed and intensive development came only after another hundred years. Now, however, it is a holiday resort with three or four miles of good clean sand forming a safe bathing-beach, as well as the usual apparatus of restaurants, amusement park and extensive parking space for cars and coaches; and on summer weekends long queues of vehicles stretch back to Havant.

SIX

Northwards from Portsmouth

The London road out of Portsmouth after leaving Cosham strikes up over a col of Portsdown Hill. At the top another road which overpasses it runs leftward along the crest on its way to Southampton, affording a wide panorama on all sides: seaward over the city to the Solent and the Isle of Wight, inland to the Hampshire downs; and then when it begins to dip towards Southwick, forward to a further vista of rolling downland beyond the distant Test valley. The immediate foreground of the inland view is diversified by patches of woodland that are surviving fragments of the Forest of Bere, which once covered the whole area between Wickham and the Sussex border and supplied fine oak timber to Portsmouth for the building of warships. At Southwick, which the road now mercifully by-passes, the priory to which the Portchester monks betook themselves in the twelfth century was converted into a country house at the Dissolution. After both this and its successor had been burnt down and replaced, the present house was taken over during the Second World War as the headquarters of General Eisenhower the Supreme Allied Commander and the final momentous decisions about the landing in France on D-Day were taken there. After the war it was transformed by modern additions in rather incongruously functional style into H.M.S. *Dryad,* the navy's school of navigation, which was now transferred thither from Portsmouth dockyard. From this cuckoo in its nest the village with its timber-framed cottages, many of them thatched, and its eighteenth-century brick houses fortunately stands somewhat apart and is therefore relatively unspoilt.

Hidden away on a side-road that leads from the Southwick bypass to

Fareham is the little Saxon church of Boarhunt (pronounced 'Borrunt'). Everything around it is completely rural; there is no village, but only two farms with long barns of brick and boarding, and it is hard to believe that Portsmouth is only just over the hill.

Meanwhile, from the crest of Portsdown the Portsmouth-London road drops again to pass through miles of ribbon development including Waterlooville, which grew up in the nineteenth century around a public-house called The Heroes of Waterloo. The story runs that it had just been built but not yet named when a detachment of troops on their march from Portsmouth, where they had just landed after the Waterloo campaign, were halted there to quench their thirst, whereupon it was decided to name the house after them.

Beyond Horndean the road climbs steadily again and presently begins to escape into open country, leaving on the left Catherington, a loosely-spaced but largely unspoilt little village forming a rural enclave in what threatens to become a solid mass of suburbia on this side of the road. Very understandably in so pleasant a place which in the past was at just the right distance from Portsmouth for an admiral's residence or retirement, it has associations with several. There is a large house that was built by Samuel Hood, one of the galaxy of great seamen of the later eighteenth century to which among others Lords Hawke and Rodney belonged. Sir Charles ('Charley') Napier, the chief naval hero of the generation after the Napoleonic War, is buried in the churchyard, and not far from his grave is a monument to the memory of Sir Christopher Cradock, who in 1914 went deliberately to his doom in a one-sided battle against long odds off Coronel in the South Pacific, hoping thereby to inflict enough damage on his enemy Von Spee to prevent him from doing further harm.

Further along on this side of the main road and at the end (so far) of the long sprawl of inter- and post-war development is Clanfield, another disjointed downland village, whose core has some old red-brick, flint, timber-framed and thatched buildings, but which is doubly spoilt by a dreadful suburban spread to its south-east and a glaringly incongruous public-house at its centre built out of prefabricated materials to replace a more harmonious predecessor. On the downs to the north is H.M.S. *Mercury*, a shore establishment that has succeeded a ship formerly moored off Hamble which trained boys for the lower decks of the navy and the merchant service. Originated in the 1880s by Charles Arthur Hoare, who provided the ship and maintained her for 23 years, the enterprise was afterwards carried on with much success and distinction by Commander C. B. Fry the famous cricketer and all-round sportsman.

On the other side of the high road from the turning down to Clanfield a side-road leads to Chalton, whose few houses are strung around a small and sloping green. Here, in addition to a largely thirteenth-century church and a former rectory of apparently medieval or at least Tudor origin with an eighteenth-century frontage, there is one of the most attractive pre-Georgian pubs in the county, not the least of whose attractions is its pleasing practice of serving elderberry, apricot, damson and other home-made wines. On top of a steep hill nearby which hides the village and the main road from each other there is a splendidly situated ruined windmill; and only when one has climbed to it and looked out westward over the countryside can one really believe that so peaceful a little place is merely a mile or so from the A30's traffic and suburban sprawl.

A little further down the dry valley on one side of which Chalton lies is Idsworth on its other side, scarcely a mile from the Sussex border. The railway from Portsmouth to London runs through this valley and when it was built the owner of the old manor-house, traces of whose foundations can be seen alongside the track, abandoned it and built a new mansion on higher ground. Not far from this and now standing alone in a field is a mainly Norman church dedicated to St Hubert, the patron saint of hunting, which contains the most important series of wall-paintings in any Hampshire church outside of Winchester, some of which are thought to depict scenes from the saint's life.

On the wooded slopes at the head of this valley is Ditcham House, the boyhood home of Captain Cowper Coles, R.N., a mid-Victorian pioneer of ironclad warship construction who, while serving in the British Black Sea Fleet at the siege of Sebastopol during the Crimean War, first caught the eye of the Admiralty by designing an effective armoured gun-raft carrying a single heavy gun in a turret. He then went on to design a type of shallow-draught armoured vessel for coastal defence, equipped with several revolving turrets, and then a sea-going ironclad similarly equipped named the *Captain*. Unhappily the low freeboard he considered necessary to give the ship almost all-round fire made her top-heavy in view of the fact that she was still a masted vessel, and in 1870 she capsized and sank in a storm off the Spanish Cape Finisterre, carrying with her Coles himself, who had sailed in her to demonstrate his faith in her stability, and all but 18 of her crew.

Over the downs from Ditcham is Buriton, which has a thirteenth-century church beside a village pond and an early Georgian manor-house in which Edward Gibbon the historian of the decline and fall of the Roman empire, who was the squire's son, spent his boyhood. In the quiet peace which the place still has and which he loved he began to develop his passion for books by browsing in his father's library, which he described as 'stuffed with old trash, High Church divinity, and politics'.

Between the turnings off the A3 which lead successively to Chalton and Buriton it passes through a great gash that has recently been hacked for it through the main southern ridge of the Hampshire downs. In doing so it runs at the foot of Butser Hill, which with a height of nearly 900 feet is the county's highest point and from which on a clear day the spire of Salisbury Cathedral 40 miles away can be seen. On the hill a most interesting enterprise has recently been begun, which has been christened the Butser Ancient Farm Research Project. This is an attempt to reconstruct as nearly as possible the farming methods and way of life of the Iron Age at approximately 300 B.C. It is based on the evidence which has been derived from excavation, the analogies which can be drawn with primitive practice surviving to-day, and such ancient documentary sources as are available. Two fields of the old Celtic type have been planted with species of primitive wheat and beans, and a variety of cereals and plants that were grown by Iron Age farmers have been sown in a hoe plot; Dexter cows and Soay sheep which approximate to the prehistoric breeds have been introduced; two round-houses modelled on evidence drawn from recent excavations at Maiden Castle and Balksbury have been built; and experiments in making pottery both in a pit clamp and in kilns are being conducted. It is hoped that this experiment in reconstruction will enable the theories drawn from excavations of Iron Age sites to be tested in a practical way.

Descending from the col at the foot of Butser, the road then comes to Petersfield, which is a medium-sized country town with a fine old square presided over by a statue of William III on horseback and in Roman costume which – though handsome in itself – has been called, because of its incongruity, the most ridiculous one in England. Originally it adorned the grounds of Petersfield House, the home of the Jolliffe family, which stood in the square until it was pulled down in 1793, after which the statue was transferred to its present position as a gift to the town. The church which stands nearby was built in the twelfth century, and in spite of some alteration and restoration remains one of the most interesting Norman ones in the county. From the square a lane leads to the little green strangely called the Spain; tradition says because dealers in Spanish wool used to hold markets there in bygone days. Here, in one of the picturesque late-seventeenth-century houses with little lattice-paned windows, lived the botanist John Goodyer who was a forerunner of Linnaeus. On one side of the town, looking towards the line of what Kipling called the 'blunt, bow-headed, whale-backed downs' that stretches away into Sussex, there is a common of 80 acres bordering a lake of 20 or more and much besprinkled with round barrows; while on the other side towards the village of Steep there is the famous Bedales School founded by J. H. Badley at the close of the nineteenth century as a protest against the formalism and narrowness of the public schools of his day. The first boarding-school for both sexes, it became the pioneer of co-education.

Above Steep loom the slopes of Stoner Hill, forming part of the hanger-clad greensand ridge that fringes the county hereabouts; and from the road that winds up to its crest as well as from the crest itself there are glorious views of the plain below and the downs fading gradually away eastward into 'the dim blue goodness of the Weald'. Here, at first in a cottage in Steep itself and then in a house on top of the hill with a summer house in the garden in which he wrote, lived the Edwardian poet Edward Thomas who was killed in the First World War. A friend of his who walked with him during his last leave from France has recorded that, when asked if he knew what he was fighting for, the poet paused a moment and then stooped to pick up a pinch of earth, saying 'I think, literally, this'. 'When he was killed in Flanders', wrote Walter de la Mare, 'a mirror of England was shattered'. There is a monument to him on the hillside, and at its unveiling the poet laureate, paying his tribute, said that Thomas had the most beautiful voice he had ever heard from human lips. Those of us who have also lived on these slopes may perhaps be pardoned for thinking this the loveliest part of all Hampshire.

The road which climbs Stoner Hill continues from its top until it joins at right angles the protraction of the Meon Valley road (the A32) which leaves the river at West Meon to run northward over a low watershed and down a dry valley to Alton. On its way this passes the villages of East Tisted and Farringdon which are pleasant or at least pleasantly situated, as well as a large castellated house called Rotherfield Park near the former village that was built in the early nineteenth century but survives only as a shell. These two roads, with that to Alton which breaks leftward from the left fork of the London road out of Petersfield as it nears Greatham, form a rough triangle that may be called the hanger country and its hinterland. Of this region Selborne is the capital. Attractively situated, it has some pretty cottages and a fine church, with impressive Norman arcades and a remarkably good Flemish triptych of the early sixteenth century, standing beside a little green called the Plestor or 'play place', where there is a gigantic yew tree.

Selborne, however, owes its fame to having been the birthplace and home of the eighteenth-century 'father of English natural history', Gilbert White. Returning to it after a promising career at Oxford and a comparatively short experience of curacies elsewhere which convinced him that he preferred Selborne's quiet and seclusion to the academic or clerical preferment he might otherwise have had, White was for more than 40 years curate (though never vicar) first here and then at Farringdon. A companionable man with friends and relatives all over southern England to whom he wrote frequently, he corresponded in particular with two other distinguished naturalists, Thomas Pennant the traveller and the lawyer Daines Barrington who is credited with having persuaded him to write his *Natural History of Selborne,* which appeared in 1789 in the form of letters to both these men. Its success was instant, thanks to White's genius for observation and description which made him a pioneer in field natural history, and it is still a classic. The Wakes, the house opposite the Plestor in which he was born and died, was acquired and endowed 20 years ago as a memorial to him. Under the aegis of the Selborne Society it is now a place of pilgrimage and conference for naturalists from far and near; while the path he created and named the Zigzag still climbs the steep hanger he made famous which overlooks the village and from which again there are wide views into Surrey and Sussex.

The fame of White, so modest and retiring in his lifetime, and of

Selborne as the Mecca of naturalists, has rather obscured the fact that from the centre of the village the gentle valley called the Lythe leads to the site of an Augustinian priory founded in 1232, where recent excavations have produced many interesting finds, the more important of which can be seen in the Curtis Museum at Alton.

In the rolling and sometimes tumbled country behind the hangers and the greensand ridge are hidden the villages of Hawkley, which is approached by lanes that are still as deep and occasionally almost as difficult as in White's day, and Newton Valence. The latter has a church that is mainly Early English though restored in 1871, as well as a 700-year-old font outside the church door, a great yew tree about seven yards round and a manor-house built in various styles whose more modern part is supposed to date from 1787. Further back towards the A32 to Alton and even more secluded are Colemore with a little Transitional-Norman and Early English church and Priors Dean which, although it is scarcely even a hamlet, has another of about the same period.

At Chawton, a village on the A32 that almost merges into Alton, Jane Austen lived most of the last years of her life and wrote her later novels, in a modest red-brick house that is now a museum in memory of her. Almost the whole of that short life was spent in Hampshire, for after leaving Steventon she spent four years at Bath and then four more at Southampton in a house in Castle Square. Since Southampton was then still in its heyday as a resort and watering-place, it may have contributed as well or even as much as Bath to her acute observation of spa society. Her family then moved to Chawton, where she lived until a short time before her death at Winchester in 1817. It was while she was living at Chawton that the three novels she had written at Steventon – *Pride and Prejudice, Sense and Sensibility* and *Northanger Abbey* – were published, and there she wrote or finished *Emma, Mansfield Park* and *Persuasion*. Some years before she came there her brother Edward had inherited Chawton House and its estate from a cousin named Knight, whose surname he adopted. The house, to and from which Jane must have walked many times, stands on the hillside overlooking the A32 and dates from the sixteenth and seventeenth centuries, but it has been much restored in a rather unattractive manner.

Rich as Hampshire was in nineteenth-century women novelists, this

15 Opposite above *The medieval Bargate at Southampton, probably the finest town gateway in the country.*

16 Opposite below *The fourteenth-century Wool House at Southampton, originally used for storing wool before shipment and now restored as the city's Maritime Museum.*

was the richest corner. At Alresford, in a house on the west side of Broad Street, Mary Russell Mitford was born in 1787, whose mother once described Jane Austen unkindly and surely most inaccurately as 'the prettiest, silliest, most affected husband-hunting butterfly'. It is to be feared that Mrs Mitford was jealous, for Jane *was* pretty and it must be admitted that her own daughter was not. Since that daughter put on record that she found Jane's work lacking in taste and in 'perception of the graceful as well as of the humorous', she may have shared some of the jealousy. But in any case Hampshire can claim only the birth and early childhood of Mary Mitford, because when she was ten years old her father, an idle and spendthrift doctor who had married an heiress and run through her fortune, moved to Three Mile Cross a few miles outside the county after winning £20,000 in a lottery (in Mary's name) which he then promptly proceeded to dissipate also; and it was there and from her knowledge of it that Mary (who had had hard work to support him) wrote her famous *Our Village*.

Another but somewhat later woman novelist than Jane Austen or Mary Mitford, Mrs Gaskell the authoress of *Cranford* and friend of the Brontës (who was, however, essentially a north-country woman), spent the later years of her life in the village of Holybourne on the other side of Alton, where she bought a house called The Lawn and died in 1865.

Alton – 'Aweltona' in the Pipe Roll for 1175 – means the town at the source of the river Wey and stands on the low watershed that separates its valley from the headwaters of the Itchen. The forest of Alice Holt (whose intriguing name is merely a corruption of Aelfsige's holt or wood and of which a few fragments still remain some miles to the east of the town) once stretched all around; and through it ran a clearing which provided a road of sorts over the Alton Pass or Gap to Farnham and the Thames. The closeness to this road of woods in which gangs of robbers could lurk, however, made the pass dangerous in medieval times, and indeed it continued to be so until well into the nineteenth century, since footpads and highwaymen used the surviving woodlands as cover down to early Victorian days.

In 1101 it was at Alton that the attempt of William the Conqueror's eldest son Duke Robert of Normandy to dispossess his brother Henry I of England collapsed when, by a treaty which was made there, Henry bought him off with 3000 marks and a mutual recognition of each other's

17 Opposite above *Timber-framed houses in Winchester Street at Botley.*

18 Opposite below *East Meon church, a veritable cathedral of the downs.*

lands. The name of Normandy Street still given to a part of Alton's main thoroughfare may just possibly reflect this event.

During the Civil War of the seventeenth century Alton saw a dramatic and gallant episode. Early in the struggle it was held for the King by a troop of horse under Lord Crawford and a small body of infantry under Colonel Richard Boles, who were surprised one dawn by an overwhelming Parliamentarian force. Crawford and the horse galloped off to Winchester for help, leaving Boles to hold out as long as he could in the hope that it might arrive in time. The Colonel fought from street to street and house to blazing house, afterwards retreating to the churchyard and then to the church with about 40 survivors of his men. Finally, when all these were dead or taken, he gained the pulpit steps and died there sword in hand with a ring of the men he had slain around him. The great door of the mainly fifteenth-century church — one of the best examples of the Perpendicular style in Hampshire — still bears the marks of Roundhead bullets which are the scars of that fight.

But Alton also has more peaceful claims to interest. According at least to the seventeenth-century antiquary John Aubrey, the great Elizabethan poet Edmund Spenser 'lived some time in these parts, in this delicate sweet air, where he ... writ a good part of his verse'; and a house in Amery Street now divided into two cottages bears a plaque claiming that this was his residence. In the latter half of the eighteenth century the town produced a doctor, William Curtis, who became a famous botanist. His manuscript lectures and notes may be seen in the museum founded in 1855 by a namesake and member of the same family, who was also a doctor but whose greatest interests were in geology and natural history generally. This was made over to the town in 1919 as part of a war memorial and is cared for by a Society of Friends of the Curtis Museum. It contains a collection of Roman and medieval antiquities, agricultural implements and documents relating to the town's history.

In the eighteenth century, too, Alton manufactured druggets and shalloons, silks and serges, bombazine and barragon (which last were respectively a twilled dress-material of worsted combined with silk or cotton and a kind of fustian). These crafts have vanished from local industry, but the brewing which also flourished in those days still survives, based on the hopfields of this part of the county. Until a few years ago it was the town's main industry, but now only one of its former three large breweries, Harp Lager, actually carries on this trade, while the other two — Watney's and Courage's — limit themselves here to bottling and distribution.

Early in the present century the population of Alton was only about 2000, but after the electrification of the railway from London it grew somewhat as a residential town. Latterly the overspill from the capital has begun to reach it, but not to anything like the same extent as at Basingstoke and Andover. Its population in 1975 was about 15,000 and on the whole it remains a pleasant and prosperous market-town, whose long winding High Street seems at first a rather jumbled mixture of old and new, but grows upon one not disagreeably.

On the western outskirts of the town is the great Treloar Hospital founded 60 years ago for crippled children by Sir William Treloar, a former London businessman and lord mayor, who prevailed upon the War Office and the Charity Commissioners to hand over a disused military hospital to form its nucleus and raised funds mainly by appealing to the City of London companies and guilds.

North-west of the town the hop-growing belt of the upper greensand, where oasthouses are almost as frequent as in Kent, extends to Bentley on the Alton-Farnham road and stretches to the south of it. Here winding lanes lead to the village of East Worldham, standing on the brink of the descent to the plain below, which has an early thirteenth-century church somewhat restored; and down to the hamlet of West Worldham, to whose church the same remarks apply. Nearby is Hartley Mauditt, which can scarcely be called even a hamlet, but whose little isolated church is mainly Norman with a rich south doorway and handsome heraldic monuments.

The left-hand fork (A325) of the London road after it leaves Petersfield runs by Greatham, near which the road through Selborne to Alton previously mentioned (B3006) takes off, and Woolmer Forest to intersect at Farnham in Surrey the A31 from Winchester through Alresford and Alton to Guildford. It then returns into Hampshire to cross the county's north-east corner at Aldershot and Farnborough; after which it plunges more permanently into Surrey to join the A30 from Winchester and Basingstoke near Camberley. Much of this branching cross-road is consecrated to the Army, both around Longmoor Camp in the wild sandy heathland of the Woolmer Forest area before it leaves Hampshire for the first time, and then more extensively at Aldershot.

Meanwhile the right-hand and main branch of this London road out of Petersfield (A3) runs through wooded country for several miles along the county boundary with Sussex, into which it ventures briefly at Hill Brow near Rake, whence there is a magnificent eastward view of most of Kipling's 'lands that lie 'twixt Rake and Rye'. Then it withdraws again to pass through Liphook, whose Royal Anchor Inn with its neighbouring chestnut tree 300 years old has housed or refreshed countless travellers between Portsmouth and the capital, among them Samuel Pepys, who was mightily relieved to find 'good honest people' keeping it after he had lost his way in the then surrounding forest, as well as Nelson and Princess Victoria, not yet queen. A few miles further on this road also definitely enters Surrey on its way to Hindhead and Guildford.

SEVEN

North
Hampshire

Broadly, the north of the county may be taken as comprising three areas: the relatively flat north-eastern corner which is partly composed of sandy heaths and pinewoods and partly of clay, and at the eastern end of which lie Aldershot and Farnborough; a central section containing Basingstoke and a group of notable country-houses; and the north-western highlands formed by the chalk ridge that runs into the county from Wiltshire near Inkpen Beacon and slopes gradually down as it nears Basingstoke, together with that part of the country at their feet which lies in Hampshire. Apart from this ridge, all this segment of the county belongs geographically and geologically to the Thames Basin, being drained or bordered by rivers that flow northward or eastward: the Loddon which rises near Basingstoke, the Blackwater that flows into it outside the county boundary after having formed the north-eastern part of that boundary for much of its course, and the Enbourne which skirts Hampshire for some miles on the north.

Aldershot, which as late as 1850 was a small village, grew into the country's chief military centre within less than a hundred years after the Crimean War had emphasized the need for Britain's soldiers to be grouped and trained during peacetime in units larger than a battalion or a brigade. Recently what used to be sometimes called its 'miles of great dreariness' have been somewhat redeemed by planned modern building, especially of a civic centre, a new town centre south of Queen's Avenue, and such establishments as the new training school for the Royal Army Nursing Corps. Farnborough, which merges imperceptibly into Aldershot and is virtually a part of it, was also a village before the coming of the

Army; but until the construction of the Royal Air Force College its chief claim to fame was that it witnessed the effective end of the long story of Napoleon. After the crushing defeat at Sedan in 1870 had brought the Second Empire of his nephew Napoleon III down in ruins the ex-Imperial family at first took refuge at Chislehurst in Kent, and it was there that the fallen Emperor died in 1873. But after his only son the Prince Imperial had been killed six years later in the Zulu War while serving in the British Army, the widowed and now childless Empress Eugénie came to Farnborough, bought and enlarged the house called Farnborough Hill (now a convent school) and lived there till her death in 1920. In 1887 she built a mausoleum in the French Flamboyant style for herself, her husband and her son, whose tombs she transferred thither. To serve the mausoleum she also built an abbey, called St Michael's, parts of which are modelled on some of the Abbey of Solesmes in Normandy.

Between Aldershot and Basingstoke are Fleet, which has been justly described as prosperous villadom and has neither shape nor character nor notable buildings; Crondall, where an avenue of lime trees leads to a church that is basically Norman and has a splendid Early English rib-vaulted chancel; and Odiham, which is one of the most attractive little towns in the county, yet with nothing self-conscious about it. Its charming High Street, whose houses are mostly eighteenth- and early nineteenth-century, has hardly a single ugly building; and its church, the largest in the north of Hampshire, contains a great deal that is interesting. Close to the church is a tiny cottage still called the Pest House, a relic of the distant days when those who were unlucky enough to catch any of the infectious diseases that were generically called the plague were bundled forthwith into some such wretched little building and probably left to their fate by family, friends and authorities alike. Near the town is the octagonal keep which is all that remains of a castle that was newly built when King John set out from it in 1215 to meet his barons at Runnymede. North Warnborough, in which parish the castle lies, is one of several pleasant villages in the neighbourhood. Others are South Warnborough whose church has one of the only two pre-Reformation rood-lofts preserved in the county, Greywell which has the other as well as a row of picturesque cottages, and Winchfield much of whose church is Norman.

Basingstoke has hitherto been dismissed by more than one writer on

Hampshire as a rather unattractive place, lacking in evidences of the past and with little in it to justify a sightseeing visit; though it has generally been admitted that the ruins of the thirteenth-century Chapel of the Holy Ghost (as it is commonly called, though the greater part of the remains are those of Holy Trinity Chapel which was added to the older one in 1542) are interesting in spite of their unfortunate proximity to the railway station. In recent times, however, it has changed greatly since Sir W. S. Gilbert in *Ruddigore* made its name a synonym for stillness and peace, having become a rapidly rising industrial town with the highest rate of growth in Britain and thus acquired an importance that demands attention.

Until after the close of the Middle Ages it was hardly more than a large village with communications that were poor even for those days, and was therefore largely dependent on its own local crafts and trades. In Tudor times, however, it gave birth by what is perhaps an intriguing coincidence to both of Hampshire's great sea-captains of that period – Robert Reneger who for his exploits against the Spaniards and in Brazil during the reign of Henry VIII (with whom he was something of a favourite) has been called Drake's predecessor, and Sir James Lancaster who first took English ships to India and beyond. By the seventeenth century it had developed a cloth industry of the kind common in little country towns; and when a canal was built towards the end of the eighteenth century to link it to the river Wey and so via the Thames to London the transport of merchandise was eased. Beyond Greywell the canal passed through a tunnel nearly a mile long, and since this stretch had no towpath the bargemen in its early days had to work their barges through by 'legging', a practice then common in such cases of lying on top of their cargo and pushing with their feet against the top of the tunnel. Only when some parts of the roof had collapsed were wheels fitted to the barges to enable them to be drawn overland to the other end. The canal, however, proved to be a marked example of the many waterways built in southern England during the 'Canal Mania' of that age which failed because they ran entirely through rural and agricultural areas and so could not attract sufficient remunerative traffic. After 40 years of struggle against a burden of debt, during which it never paid a dividend, it received a mortal blow when the London and Southampton Railway (which soon became the London and South-Western) was opened to

Basingstoke in 1839. After the original canal company had gone into liquidation, several abortive attempts at revival were made, including one in recent years, which has now been abandoned, to use the canal for carrying pleasure traffic.

Until some distance into the twentieth century — as long, in fact, as British industries were largely bound to the coal and iron fields of the north and northern midlands — Basingstoke remained a sleepy agricultural centre. Then it began to grow, especially during and after the Second World War. By 1951 it had a population of 17,000 and was largely engaged in manufacture, with motor works, engineering shops, metal foundries and an important pharmaceutical company's plant. Ten years later its all-important Town Development Scheme was agreed on jointly by the London County Council (now the Greater London Council), the Hampshire County Council and the Borough Council (now the Basingstoke District Council). By this it was proposed to expand the town by building approximately 11,500 houses (later reduced to 9250) for Londoners by about 1976; the object being to give them better opportunities for housing, education, employment and recreation, and at the same time help to curb the growth of London's population and area. The division of functions between the three authorities was and is that the L.C.C. (now the G.L.C.) should find firms in London willing to move to Basingstoke with most of their employees and should nominate the latter, together with other persons finding work in Basingstoke or otherwise suitable, as tenants for houses erected under the scheme; the County Council as the overall planning authority for the region should provide the necessary roads, schools, libraries, medical and other social service facilities; and the Borough (now District) Council would buy the land needed for development, manage all dwellings once they were completed, and provide recreational, community and other normal municipal services.

By 1974 more than 80 firms had moved into the industrial estates created by the Council, most of them coming from London though some were local firms which wished to expand on new and better sites and had benefited by being able to obtain labour from London; nearly 9000 houses had been provided for both Londoners and local people as well as over 3600 built by local enterprise keeping pace with town development building; 31,000 people had moved to Basingstoke under the scheme; the population, which had been 26,000 in 1961, was estimated at

63,000; and it is expected that with a few surrounding villages it will reach 113,000 by 1986.

The face of the town has also been transformed. A pedestrian-only shopping centre with the shops grouped in squares and enclosed courts and including also flats, offices and a public library has been built and is to be extended; and on the east side of it a new market square has been constructed. A major road now runs through the middle of the town, linking at each end with a ring-road, two-thirds of which is completed and which will be six miles long when finished. Parks, recreation grounds and playing-fields have been plentifully provided. Much of what has been or is being built in industrialized or 'rationalized traditional' style is of a respectable or passable architectural standard, though unhappily the making of the new shopping centre has involved the destruction of many of what were Basingstoke's best houses and the rows of monotonously uniform boxlike dwellings on some of its outskirts are sadly dreary. Nevertheless it has become an industrial town without the horrors usually associated with such; its houses are clean and there is very little smoke. It is therefore not hard to understand why its people, including that majority of them whom its industries have drawn in from London and other parts of the country, are proud of it.

Two miles east of Basingstoke lies Basing, with the ruins of what was once one of the greatest houses in the country, which withstood a famous siege during the Civil War. It was built by Sir William Paulet, one of the Tudors' 'new men', who became the first Marquess of Winchester and was adviser to four out of the five Tudor monarchs. His descendant the fifth Marquess fortified and garrisoned it for Charles I and stood off a succession of attacks for three years until in 1645 Cromwell himself, fresh from the capture of Winchester, came and laid siege to it. The improbable legend that the success of his storming-parties early one morning was due to surprising some of the defenders playing cards gave rise to the old Hampshire saying 'Clubs are trumps, as when Basing House was taken'. Since the Marquess and many of the garrison were Catholics little quarter was given, though among the survivors was the great architect Inigo Jones, who is said to have been stripped and carried out in a blanket. 'Loyalty House', as it had deservedly been called, was then reduced to ruins, though the Marquess, who was henceforth known as 'the great loyalist', was allowed to leave the country after a period of imprisonment in the Tower and lived in exile till the Restoration.

His eldest son and successor was evidently something of a contrast to his father, since in Charles II's reign he took the other side in politics and strongly supported the Whig opposition, having abandoned the Catholic faith. This placed him in jeopardy under Charles's successor, the Catholic James II, but he saved himself by feigning madness, spending his time in riding around the country with a considerable entourage, hunting by night and sleeping by day. After actively supporting William of Orange on his landing to supplant James he was created Duke of Bolton, though it is hardly surprising that even the Whig Bishop Burnet described him as 'a very crafty politic man'. In 1683-7 he had built Hackwood Park a mile or two south of Basingstoke, which was remodelled by James Wyatt's nephew Lewis at the beginning of the nineteenth century. Though grand in scale it is unfortunately cement-rendered. The most interesting feature of the park is Spring Wood, a formal layout of about a century earlier than that, with a centre and eight radiating avenues consisting wholly of yew trees.

A greater and more splendid house, which like Basing owed its origin to one of the Tudor new nobility, is The Vyne near Sherborne St John, where about three miles north of Basingstoke the open chalk hills of central Hampshire suddenly give place to the wooded valley of the Loddon. It was built early in Henry VIII's reign by his Lord Chamberlain Lord William Sandys, on a site chosen for shelter rather than strength (as by then great houses often were), with the ground rising gently from it on all sides and a tributary of the Loddon running through its park. After the Civil War it was purchased from the now rather impoverished Sandys family (who then withdrew to their other property of Mottisfont Abbey near Romsey) by Chaloner Chute, a distinguished lawyer who became Speaker of the House of Commons towards the end of the Commonwealth period. Under him it received extensive alterations and additions, as it did again in the later eighteenth century under his descendant John Chute, who fortunately managed to resist the wild suggestions for improvement made by his friend Horace Walpole. After remaining in the possession of the family for 300 years — though as in similar cases elsewhere this apparent continuity was partly due to its twice passing to a distant relative of another name who then assumed that of Chute — it was left to the National Trust by Sir Charles Chute in 1956.

Its chapel, for which the first Lord Sandys was responsible, is probably the best private medieval one in England. Rich in pictures, china and furniture, it includes among its minor treasures one which was formerly thought to be the subject of a remarkable coincidence. This is a gold Roman ring found locally in 1786 and bearing the inscription 'Seniciane vivas in deo', which may be translated 'O Senicianus, mayest thou live in God's keeping'. The apparent coincidence was that a small leaden tablet was afterwards found among the ruins of a Romano-British temple at Lydney in Gloucestershire which advertised the loss of a ring which was taken to be this one, since it invoked curses on one Senicianus until he should restore it. Unfortunately more modern scrutiny and a consideration of dates show that the ring at The Vyne cannot be that lost at Lydney, since the former is fourth-century work and its inscription was a Christian formula common in that age, while the Lydney tablet belongs to the first or at latest second century and the name Senicianus was not uncommon.

A few miles beyond The Vyne and on the northern verge of the county are two more great houses, Stratfield Saye and Bramshill. The former place got its name from the Roman road (or 'street') that ran from London through Silchester to Bath, which here forms the county boundary, and from the fact that it was once owned by a De Saye family; and the original unimpressive house (set however in a magnificent park) was built probably in the seventeenth century. It owes its celebrity to the fact that after the battle of Waterloo it was bought and presented by a grateful nation to the Duke of Wellington, who added the outer wings on the west or entrance front and to whom there is a towering monument in the park. Naturally it is full of relics of the great Duke, and has recently been thrown open to the public daily during August and September. The park is also open on certain days as a leisure centre. Bramshill, an early Tudor-Jacobean mansion worthy to rank with Hatfield and Holland House (indeed, the same man built all three) has a wonderful setting on a hill which dominates the countryside amid rolling parkland, bracken-clad heath and woods, and is reached by an avenue a mile long. Being now a police college, however, it is not open to the public.

This corner of the county has associations with several of the great Hampshire families of bygone centuries. Besides the Paulets there were the St Johns after whom Sherborne St John is named, and the De Port

family, a member of which in 1110 divided the manor of Sherborne and
gave half of it to a Benedictine priory he founded at Pamber near what
therefore came to be called Monk Sherborne a mile or two away on the
other side of the Basingstoke-Aldermaston road. In the fifteenth century
this priory came into the hands of God's House at Southampton, which
itself was by then owned by Queen's College, Oxford, and the College
still maintains the church which is all that is left of it and whose massive
tower still dominates the scene. From Monk Sherborne, which also has a
mainly Norman church of its own, an avenue of oaks leads through fields
to the priory church, which has experienced two restorations in fairly
modern times. Not far away and even nearer to The Vyne is Beaurepaire,
the ancient moated manor-house of the Brocas family; but despite its
attractive name what is left of it after a serious fire a generation ago is of
little architectural interest. Nearby is Eversley, of which Charles Kingsley
was rector for thirty-one years until his death in 1875. Far from devoting
himself entirely or mainly to his novels, he worked tirelessly for his
parishioners and with them too in the fields at harvest-time, transforming
what had been a rough and tough parish neglected by his predecessor. He
was so beloved that when he died he had such a funeral as perhaps no
country parson ever had before or since.

In this corner of the county, too, there are three churches well worth a
visit: Nately Scures, a little Norman gem; Mattingley, late medieval and
timber-framed throughout with infilling of brick-nogging between the
timbers; and Yateley, with a Norman nave and early thirteenth-century
chancel both sensitively restored and a fifteenth-century tower that is also
timber-framed.

A few miles west of Stratfield Saye is Silchester, the site of the
Romano-British town of Calleva Atrebatum, deserted now save for a
church and a farm. Its founders the Atrebates were a tribe living during
the first century B.C. in northern Gaul, where Arras still preserves their
name, and a section of which emigrated to Britain about the middle of
that century. Since they evidently established Calleva soon afterwards it
was thus, like Venta, in existence before the coming of the Romans,
though perhaps more briefly. As is implied by its Celtic name, which is
related to the Welsh *celli* meaning 'wood', it was set among woods of
which the nearby Pamber Forest is a surviving remnant, though on a
gravel spur about 300 feet above sea-level which would be more easily

cleared for building and cultivation. Since the only level access is from the west, the site had considerable defensive advantages. It was extensively excavated between 1864 and 1909, and again in 1954-8 by Mr George Boon, who has written an excellent book about it and also a still more up-to-date brochure which is on sale at the little museum near Silchester rectory to the west of the town walls.

From this museum, erected in 1951 as a contribution to the Festival of Britain and to which entry is free, a footpath leads after a third of a mile to the walls near what was once the west gate. The main though also somewhat difficult approach, however, is to the east gate by rather narrow roads either from the village of Stratfield Mortimer to the north-east or Mortimer West End to the north, or alternatively from Bramley to the south. At present (1976) there is no public access to the walls, since work is being carried out under the Ministry of Public Building and Works to make them safe, but as it proceeds consolidated sections will be opened to visitors. The fine collection of archaeological material which was obtained from the successive excavations is housed in Reading Museum and is merely epitomized in the tiny museum on the spot. The building foundations which had been revealed, of which the most intriguing were those of what is generally taken to have been a small Christian church dating from very late in the Roman period, were covered over again, since to preserve them in an exposed state would have been very costly and in any case the 107 acres within the walls are the best arable of the above-mentioned farm. Nothing is therefore visible within these walls except a vast field cut by traces of what had been the town's two principal streets; though on the east side the amphitheatre that was a usual feature of Roman provincial towns remains apparent.

Like Venta again, though to a lesser extent, Calleva was a road-centre, and from its gateways four roads radiated. Neither that going north to Dorchester-on-Thames nor that which went west to Speen can now be followed; nor can the first part of that southwards to Venta, though this can be picked up at Sherborne St John and followed more or less through Worting to the point near North Waltham where it merges into the long straight stretch of the Winchester-Basingstoke road already mentioned. The road going south-west to Old Sarum is marked on the maps as the Portway running from Silchester over the Wiltshire border, but in practice it also cannot be seen for its first few miles over the lower land before the chalk escarpment of the North Hampshire Downs is reached. It is best picked up by taking the road from Kingsclere south over White Hill, a mile or so beyond which a long line of trees called Caesar's Belt comes in from the north-east with the Portway clearly visible as a raised causeway. Even so, it cannot be followed continuously afterwards but only discovered here and there, as at St Mary Bourne and again at Hundred Acre Corner just beyond Andover on the Devizes road.

These North Hampshire Downs, most of which are still a walker's paradise, begin gently near Basingstoke, where an Iron Age fort at Winklebury has now been swallowed up in the expanding town; though it is really only at White Hill that the first stretch of splendid walking starts. Here about 600 feet up on the thin dry tufted grass or sometimes the bare chalk there is hardly a human being to be met, and the walker looks down on the plain stretching away to the Thames or across to the Berkshire Downs beyond the Vale of Kennet. From White Hill — a particularly fine viewpoint — he passes to Watership Down, which has given its name to Richard Adams' delightful fantasy about a rabbit colony on the down; a story that already rivals Kenneth Grahame's *The Wind in the Willows* and will, like it, become a classic for children and adults alike. Next comes Ladle Hill, on which there is a fort that the Iron Age builders left unfinished, thereby enabling us to see the stages by which this and presumably other similar strongholds were constructed. Apparently they began by digging a small marking-out ditch, traces of which can be seen in the north-eastern part of the site, to indicate the line of the subsequent defensive ditch on which work then started. The topsoil and turf from this were carried some distance inside the fort to be dumped — these topsoil dumps can still be seen as irregular mounds — and the chalk rubble from further down in the ditch was piled behind it to form a solid core for the rampart. The final stage would have been the capping of this core by bringing back the turf and topsoil from the dumps, but at this point the whole work was abandoned for some reason that can only be conjectured.

On Beacon Hill, on the far side of the cleft in the escarpment where the Winchester-Newbury road comes over, there is another hill fort, and at Walbury Hill a few miles further on there is yet another which encloses an area almost half-a-mile wide. However both Walbury and Inkpen Beacon a mile beyond it (which at almost a thousand feet is the highest point of these downs) are now in Berkshire, a little enclave of which runs up over them to take in the village of Combe; though till less than a hundred years ago they were in Hampshire, to which they surely belong geographically. The reason for the transfer was an administrative one; the fact that owing to the difficulty of the roads between Combe and Andover it was decided that Hungerford in the Kennet Valley would be a more convenient centre for rating and similar purposes.

The capital (if such a term can be applied to a place that hovers uncertainly between being a village and a little town) of the small segment of Hampshire that lies north of these downs is Kingsclere, a sleepy little spot with a church which contains some fine Norman work but has been rather over-restored. Burghclere nearby also has a church with Norman elements, but its most notable building is the Sandham Memorial Chapel that commemorates the memory of a young officer who died in 1919 from an illness contracted in Macedonia during the 1914-18 war. On its walls the Expressionist painter Stanley Spencer, who had spent part of the war as a hospital orderly and later went to Macedonia, was commissioned to paint a cycle of pictures which are starkly realistic. The third 'clere' (the derivation of the final syllable of these three names is uncertain) is Highclere, where in a park that was the work of Capability Brown and is one of the loveliest in southern England stands an early Victorian castle which is the home of the Earls of Carnarvon and the largest mansion in Hampshire.

EIGHT

Coming Down
the Test

To anglers the Test is the most famous of all the chalk streams of the south country, which are to them what the shires are to the hunting man; and its fame for trout fishing extends far beyond Britain to all the corners of the world. There is salmon fishing too, or there was; but it was confined to the lower reaches of the river between Romsey and Redbridge and pollution has practically killed it now.

The Test has of course been fished since time immemorial, but it was in the early part of the nineteenth century that two famous clubs were formed on it: the Leckford Club, which held a very fine stretch of the river above Stockbridge, and the Houghton Club (pronounced 'Howton') which had a ten-mile length immediately below the Leckford water. The headquarters of this celebrated, exclusive and expensive club are the Grosvenor Hotel at Stockbridge, where the walls of its clubroom are lined with cases containing colossal stuffed trout. But to fish the best reaches of the Test at all regularly one has to be a very wealthy man; and even so, the fishing is occasionally though perhaps erroneously said to be no longer what it once was, because the river is overfished.

But if its greatest fame is as the close fishing preserve of the wealthy few, it is a charming river in itself and runs through rich and pleasant country. It rises near Ashe, a hamlet just off the Andover-Basingstoke road a mile or two east of Overton, at which latter place that road is joined by another coming boldly southward over the downs from Kingsclere. Like Alresford at the source of the Itchen, Overton consists of a village with a church and a manor-house on one side of the fledgling river and a newer town built by Bishop de Lucy of Winchester on the other side; but its wide main street is not as straight and impressive as Alresford's and it is a sadly decayed place. Once it was a busy market town and one of the first Hampshire boroughs to be represented in Parliament, with an important sheep and lamb fair and silk mills that have now vanished. It was also the end of the first coaching stage from London, with 60 horses in the stables of the Poyntz Arms which then stood at the crossroads where the schools are now, ready to supply fresh teams for the coaches or relays for posting. But when coach travel was killed by the railway it lapsed into insignificance.

Even before the Test reaches Overton it has begun to show its peculiar characteristic of splitting into a number of separate channels. By the time that it has run ten miles it has become a river of considerable size, though it still sometimes divides again into several branches, while at other times it runs as one stream over magnificent open shallows. A little lower down the river than Overton is Laverstoke, where for two and a quarter centuries the Bank of England notes were manufactured. This manufacture was developed here by Henri Portal, a member of a prominent Huguenot family of Toulouse who had been brought to Southampton as a boy among the refugees who formed the French Church there. According to tradition he and his brother had been hidden in an oven by an old nurse when Louis XIV's soldiers came to seize the family château, and afterwards smuggled on board a lugger by faithful friends and servants. When Henri grew up he found work at a mill at South Stoneham a little to the north of Southampton where papermaking was carried on under the management of another Frenchman. While learning the trade from this man he met and became friendly with that same Sir William Heathcote who had bought the Hursley estate from Richard Cromwell's daughters. From him he obtained the lease of Bere Mill near Whitchurch and set up a paper manufactory there (having become a naturalised Englishman), which he transferred a few years later to a neighbouring mill at Laverstoke. In 1727 he secured from Sir Gilbert Heathcote, the Governor of the Bank of England and uncle of his friend Sir William, the contract for the manufacture of the Bank's notes, since the water of the Test apparently has a quality which pre-eminently fits it for making the crisp paper needed for this purpose. In 1950, however, the manufacture of the notes was transferred to another mill on the northern outskirts of Overton, beside the railway station. Meanwhile

Henri's descendants, among the more recent of whom was the late Marshal of the Royal Air Force Lord Portal, one of the great figures of the Battle of Britain, have become a leading Hampshire family.

Two miles further down the river is Whitchurch, another little town whose glories have departed. Like Overton it once had a large market and returned two members to Parliament, and travellers to or from Newbury or Oxford joined or left the Exeter coach there. To-day it is a little better known than Overton only because it stands on the Winchester-Newbury road. Its White Hart Hotel was formerly one of the best in the county but is now closed, probably because of the threat to its trade presented by a new-built bypass round the town. Below it the river skirts Hurstbourne Park, where the mansion of the Earls of Portsmouth stood until it was pulled down in 1965. It then receives on its right bank its first tributary, the Bourne, which rises in the downland of the north-west corner of the county near Hurstbourne Tarrant.

A short mile south of this latter village, on the main Andover-Newbury road that here crosses the Bourne valley, a minor road on the right past Doles Wood climbs up three miles to Tangley, affording splendid views all the way. As it nears Tangley it intersects the built-up causeway of the old Roman road from Winchester to Cirencester, which can then be followed rightwards to the vantage-point called Hampshire Gate on the Wiltshire border. Tangley, a well-situated hilltop village which nevertheless lacks architectural distinction, used to be considered the remotest and most isolated of all in these parts. Its occasional designation in former days of 'God-forsaken Tadley' (for so its name was pronounced locally) derives, according to a story that may be *ben trovato,* from an occurrence 80 years ago when a balloonist made a forced landing in a cottager's garden and asked him where he was. The cottager, taking him from the manner of his arrival to be a most celestial Personage, fell on his knees and cried 'Oh Lord God Almighty, forgive us, for this is God-forsaken Tadley!' There is perhaps more credence to be attached to William Cobbett's report of meeting there a woman of about 30 who had never been more than two and a half miles from the village and could not tell him the way to Ludgershall four miles off.

Hurstbourne Tarrant itself, the second element of whose name derives from the fact that in 1266 Henry III gave the manor to Tarrant Abbey in Dorset as part of its endowment, is a village of which Cobbett was very fond, staying there frequently with his friend Joseph Blount at Rookery Farm House. In the middle of the front garden wall of the house is a brick incised 'W.C. 1825' which commemorates this, since it was then a masons' tradition when a wall or house was built to invite some notable person to lay an incised brick and pay a footing. The church, which is transitional between Norman and Early English, contains some much faded and indistinct medieval mural paintings on the north wall of the nave. One of these is a *memento mori* representing the legend of 'The Three Living and the Three Dead', according to which three kings out hunting in a forest met three skeletons who reminded them that even they must also die. Another mural, representing the Seven Deadly Sins, is too faint to be deciphered in detail. On the northward road out of the village is the Bladon Gallery, embracing crafts as well as pictures, which is well worth a visit; and at Ibthorpe, which merges into the village on the Vernham Dean road north-westward, there is a charming small manor-house of the Queen Anne period.

In the coaching era Hurstbourne Tarrant had a large number of inns, one suggested reason being that the coaches needed to change horses before tackling the steep hill on its south side; but of these inns only the George and Dragon survives today. Nevertheless one could do much worse than spend a long summer weekend or even a week there, since from the village there are excellent walks and drives through a sparsely populated and unspoilt countryside with pleasant secluded villages such as Upton, Vernham Dean and Linkenholt to the north-west.

Below Hurstbourne Tarrant the Bourne flows through a wide and attractive valley past St Mary Bourne and Hurstbourne Priors, neither of which comes up to the expectations their names might arouse, though the former's church has another of Hampshire's black Tournai marble fonts.

After its junction with the Bourne the Test passes the picturesque and aptly named village of Longparish sprawling along beside one of the loveliest reaches of the river. Here in the charming manor-house in the nineteenth century lived Colonel Peter Hawker, author of a shooting classic, *Instructions to Young Sportsmen in all that Relates to Guns and Shooting*. In his sixteenth year Hawker, who served later in the Peninsular War and then became a Lieutenant-colonel in the Hampshire Militia, had formed the habit of keeping a diary in which he recorded his shooting exploits and which provided much of the material for his *magnum opus*.

Fine shot though he undoubtedly was, however, it has been suggested that his marksmanship included some proficiency in drawing the long bow. His grandaughter Marie, who lived at Hurstbourne Priors in later life, wrote a number of stories and articles under the pseudonym of Lanoe Falconer, in which with much humour and insight she produced studies of village characters.

Below Longparish the Test flows past all that is left of Harewood Forest, which once spread for miles around and was a favourite hunting-ground of Saxon kings. It is still wild enough to provide some delightful and solitary walks. Then comes Wherwell (pronounced 'Hurrell'), a pretty village with many thatch-and-plaster cottages at the foot of a steep hill. Here, in the tenth century, Elfrida the widow of King Edgar the Peaceful founded a nunnery of which scarcely a stone survives, in remorse for arranging the murder of her stepson Edward in order to secure the throne for her own child Ethelred, afterwards to be known as the Unready.

A mile or so further down-river the next tributary, the Anton, comes in from Andover, the natural capital of north-west Hampshire, which is experiencing the same expansion and transformation as Basingstoke, though on a somewhat smaller scale. From being a small country town which was sometimes said to be so quiet that the dogs lying on the pavement opened their eyes in surprise if anyone passed by, it is growing into a busy if minor centre of industry and commerce. In 1961 its borough council entered, at the same time and on the same lines as Basingstoke's, into an agreement with what was then the London County Council and with the Hampshire County Council by which it was to become an 'expanded' town and accept surplus population and industry from the London area. Its population was then 15,000; it is now (1976) more than double that figure, and a further increase to 48,000 by 1981 is planned. Meanwhile under the reorganisation of local government it ceased in 1974 to be a municipal borough and became part of the Test Valley District along with its own former rural district, plus that of Romsey and Stockbridge and the former borough of Romsey.

Among the industries which have moved into the town and for which new factory estates have been and are being provided are printing, light and general engineering, vehicle body-building, milling, woodworking, clothing and electronics. Large housing estates, new schools, roads, and a new town centre involving the transformation of the former main shopping street into a traffic-free pedestrian area have been built. The loss of the town's old character and many of its once-familiar landmarks which all this has meant is viewed with regret by some of the native inhabitants; but it is still a pleasant place in which to live. One outstanding landmark which survives is the church, strikingly situated on a hill above the new central area. Built in the 1840s at the expense of a retired headmaster of Winchester College who had come to live in Andover, it is a remarkable building with an impressive exterior and a positively sensational interior.

Until Andover ceased to be a borough in its own right another survival, with a longer history than the fine but relatively modern church, was the ancient and latterly honorific office of ale-taster, whose function in times past had been to taste the local brew and to report beer which was below standard and licensed victuallers who were selling short measure. To help him in the former task he was at one time provided with a pair of leather breeches, and one test of the brews he sampled was to pour some on a wooden seat and sit in it. If he stuck to the seat at all it was below par; but if he rose freely it was fit for human consumption.

Three miles beyond Andover on the main west road is Weyhill, once famous for a fair second only to St Giles's at Winchester. It was already declining when Cobbett wrote of it in his *Rural Rides* in 1822 and 1826, though sixty years later Thomas Hardy in *The Mayor of Casterbridge* presented it under a thin disguise as the fair at which the drunken hay-tresser Michael Henchard sold his wife and child to a sailor for five guineas. Though still held with some liveliness in mid-October it is now a mere shadow of its former self, especially since it was a sheep fair and sheep are of no great consequence in England today. Further west again, on and near the Amesbury road into Wiltshire are Thruxton, where a Roman villa was discovered which contained a fine mosaic now in the British Museum depicting Bacchus riding on a tiger, and Quarley with a Saxo-Norman church and an Iron Age fort on a tree-capped hill nearby.

Two or three miles north of Andover on the Newbury road is a village formerly called Knights Enham where in 1919 a village centre was founded by a charitable trust to provide homes and work for disabled ex-servicemen of the First World War. In 1945, after a quarter of a million pounds had been donated for its expansion by the Egyptian people, who wished to provide a memorial that would express their gratitude for their deliverance from the Axis Powers by the victory of El Alamein, the village was rechristened Enham Alamein. This Egyptian gift allowed a number of additional cottages for disabled tenants to be built, and in the forecourt of these now stand the bell and nameplate from the railway station of El Alamein, while the gates of one of the hostels were once those of the Alamein Club in Cairo. These hostels are for the accommodation of single men and for patient-trainees during rehabilitation. There are over 150 cottages for those able to live here with their families, as well as workshops, a village hall, playing-fields and shops. The industries include light engineering, cabinet-making, carpentry and upholstery.

A little south of Andover the Anna stream joins the Anton, passing on its way the pleasant village of Abbotts Ann, whose name derives from an older variant of that of the stream, together with the fact that it once belonged to Newminster Abbey at Winchester. In the early eighteenth century the lord of the manor was Thomas ('Diamond') Pitt, the grandfather of the great prime minister William Pitt the Elder. Thomas owed his nickname to the greatest of the *coups* by which he had enriched himself in India, the purchase for £20,000 of the Pitt Diamond which he later sold for £135,000. Here a funeral custom lingers that was once common in many Hampshire villages, by which when spinsters or bachelors young or old die their coffins are accompanied to the grave by persons carrying a white chaplet or 'virginal crown' and a pair of large white gloves on a wand. The chaplet and gloves are then hung up in the church, on either side of the nave of which a full row of them survives, mostly dark with age; though there are a few comparatively recent sets, the latest of which at the moment is dated 1973. After leaving Abbotts Ann the Anna then passes below the Iron Age fort on Bury Hill, which is believed to have been intermittently occupied until the end of the first century A.D.

A few miles below the junction of the Anton with the Test is the tiny town of Stockbridge, which has an attractive street flanked by mellow Tudor and Georgian houses but with nothing very much behind them on either side. It was once the rottenest of all the parliamentary rotten boroughs in the county, with the possible exception of Newtown in the Isle of Wight. The story goes that when Richard Steele, the playwright who in Queen Anne's reign conducted the *Tatler* and the *Spectator* in association with Addison, was canvassing the town, he promised an apple stuffed with guineas to the first elector who should have an addition to his family nine months after his election. Since he was not elected, however, he did not have to keep this promise. What is more definitely established is that in 1790 two candidates spent £10,000 apiece on one election. Until the beginning of this century the town was also a famous racing centre where the Market Room in the Grosvenor Hotel used to ring with the revelries of gentlemen riders.

Close to Stockbridge on east and west respectively, on the downs above the river, are two more hill forts, Woolbury and Danebury. Woolbury with its height of 521 feet has the finer view, but Danebury with its three lines of ramparts and ditches was clearly the more important. Its inner rampart, rising 32 feet from the much-silted ditch in front of it, is the biggest in the south of England after those of Old Sarum and Maiden Castle. Beyond Danebury are the attractive villages of Upper, Middle and Nether Wallop on the Wallop Brook, whose peculiar name merely derives disappointingly from the Old English 'wiell-hop' — 'valley of the stream'. Broughton, lower down it, has a fine church and a friendly inn. On the other side of the Test, which hereabouts breaks into two and then three interlacing channels and becomes a river of special charm, are the Sombornes, Kings and Little, with an interesting old cruck cottage on the road between them. Kings Somborne is a pleasant village whose houses are mainly grouped round a small green, and Little Somborne has a Saxo-Norman church.

A return to the Test leads to the lovely Mottisfont Abbey. In or about 1201 there was founded here a small house of Augustinian Canons who had chosen this gentle valley sheltered from what was then the bleak and savage country around and plentifully supplied with water and fish. (A spring or 'font' rising into a deep pool near the house, at which the Saxons of the village used to hold their moots, is thought to be the origin of the name.) This priory was suppressed at the dissolution of the monasteries and acquired by Lord Sandys at the same time as The Vyne. The work of transforming it into a residence which he began was continued by his two successors, though (unusually in such cases) they carved the resultant mansion not so much out of the residential parts of the priory, which was largely demolished, as out of its church. Afterwards the Tudor house they had made was transmuted into a mid-eighteenth-century mansion by the Mills family into whose hands it had passed through a female. In 1957 it was given to the National Trust with an endowment by the last owner, who had had the drawing-room decorated and transformed into a Gothic *trompe-l'oeil* fantasy by Rex Whistler – the last room to be decorated by Whistler before he was killed in the Second World War.

At East Tytherley among the secluded byways behind Mottisfont the disciples of Robert Owen, the factory owner who turned social reformer and then pioneer socialist, established in the 1840s Harmony Hall, one of the short-lived communistic communities which were based on his ideas. After the frailties of humanity had proved fatal to the enterprise the house became an agricultural college under the more non-committal name of Queenwood and later a school.

A mile or so north of Romsey, as the road crosses Great Bridge, there is a delightful glimpse of a short reach of the river, with Greatbridge House set among trees. Romsey itself is a market town which is not strikingly attractive apart from an abbey that lifts it altogether out of the commonplace. A nunnery was founded here by Alfred the Great's son and successor Edward for his daughter but was sacked by the Danes, and the great church we see is Norman and Early English, most of it due to the ubiquitous Bishop Henry de Blois of Winchester. At the Dissolution it was bought by the town when most other conventual buildings were pulled down and thus was saved from demolition. The finest church in Hampshire and perhaps in all the south of England, it dwarfs the modern buildings huddled around it – especially to those who approach the town by the road from the New Forest over the hill above the broad and wooded valley. Its interior is sheer flawless beauty, of perfect proportion; Norman work unequalled throughout the country. There is also in the town a medieval house in Church Court which is called King John's Hunting-Lodge and is said to be the house in which his daughter Joanna lived with her governess before she married the King of Scotland, and which was then given to the Abbey as a guest-house. In addition the town has a noted brewery (Strong's), corn and paper mills, and ironworks.

On the southern outskirts of Romsey lies Broadlands, the birthplace of Lord Palmerston whose statue stands in the town's market-square and now the home of Earl Mountbatten. The present house is the result of the alteration of an earlier one by Capability Brown in the 1760s. Politics kept Palmerston away from it for many years, but whenever he could manage to do so he loved to get down there for a run with the New Forest hounds or a day's shooting. At East Wellow a few miles to the north-west is Embley Park, the home and burial-place of Florence Nightingale, though in her youth most of her summers were spent at her other home in Derbyshire and after her achievements in the Crimea had made her famous she lived mostly as an invalid on her couch in South Street, Mayfair.

At Nursling three miles below Romsey was the monastery from which in the eighth century St Boniface (whose baptismal name was Winfrith) went to convert the Germans to Christianity. This, however, was later destroyed by the Danes. Nursling's great house is Grove Place, now a school and at the moment (1976) a little difficult of access because of large-scale road reconstruction, but open to the public on summer Sundays. It is a typical early Elizabethan mansion, built in brick at a time of energetic building when the 'new men' enriched by the looted lands of the monasteries wanted to make as big a display of their wealth as possible. It was the time too when the new fashion for glass led to the construction of oriel windows to look out over the formal gardens that had also come into vogue. The house, which is one of the most attractive small Tudor mansions in all Wessex with its lovely façade, its windows and its beautiful gardens, was built by James Pagett, a London merchant's son who had had his share of the plunder of the abbeys. With its fine plasterwork ceilings, oak panelling and noble staircase (for another fashion which had just come in was the development of the staircase as a display of grandeur) it is a good example of the style of building that suited the fancy of this rising class of merchants turned landowners. In the eighteenth century Georgian additions were made at each end of the house. Approached by an avenue of lofty lime trees, it is a lovely sight when the daffodil terraces are ablaze with gold.

A mile or two eastward from Nursling is Rownhams, now almost swallowed up by Southampton. In its churchyard a tombstone somewhat strangely inscribed 'God be merciful to me a sinner (by request)' marks the grave of a man who might be called the other Neville Chamberlain; though while the prime minister was a man of peace this was a soldier who had served long and gallantly in India and Afghanistan and then come back at last to spend his retirement in Rownhams as a field-marshal.

Though widely recognised as among the bravest of the brave, he felt at times a strong revulsion from what he once called his cruel profession, and this may have been responsible for his self-chosen epitaph. In his prime he had been a noted swordsman, and it is recorded that once when he was waylaid by roughs while walking home by night across Shirley Common he promptly set about them with his stick and put them to flight.

Below Nursling on the Test is Redbridge, already mentioned, where the river swells into Southampton Water.

NINE

The New Forest

Most people think of a forest as an extensive tract of woodland, and in fact the New Forest does contain a number of such tracts. Indeed a rather naïve Russian lady who was once told that I lived there at the time immediately exclaimed 'But are you not afraid of wolves?'! The original meaning of the word 'forest', however, was merely a stretch of uncultivated country, and in medieval England a forest was a definite tract of such country within which a particular body of law called the forest law was enforced in order to secure the preservation of certain wild animals, especially deer for the king's hunting. There are still a number of nominal forests in England, but only the New Forest has retained anything much of its original character and it is fully in keeping with that character that a good deal of it consists of moorland, though without any of the climatic rigours commonly associated therewith.

The idea that this whole region was laid waste by William the Conqueror to create a hunting forest, though based on the statements of contemporary chroniclers, is now discredited. It was already a royal hunting-ground in Canute's day, and all that William did was to confirm its hitherto informal status in strict legal form, enlarge its boundaries and place it under a drastic code of forest law. Since the chroniclers were almost all clergy angered by the tighter hold the Norman monarchs had taken over the Church and some of them were also members of the defeated Saxon race, they naturally presented a biassed view of these proceedings, placing on record harrowing tales of 60 churches cast down, fertile villages made desolate, forced migrations of the people and so forth. But the evidence shows that these tales were exaggerations and misrepresentations. Domesday Book names 108 places in the Forest, of which about 30, covering altogether approximately 17,000 acres, were thrown entirely into it; removed, that is, from settlement actual or potential and added to the pre-existing royal preserves. Geology and the nature of the soil as it remains to-day show clearly that most of these 30 could never have been fertile ploughland nor have supported a numerous population. In many of the rest only the woodlands and wastes lying out from the settled centres were interfered with, no doubt to prevent the further enlargement or closer settlement of these centres. As for the churches, the sworn testimony of elders on which Domesday was based does not suggest the previous existence of even half as many as 60 in the whole district. In many cases, too, even comparatively prominent tenants of the land such as Aelfric, the thane of Brockenhurst, were not dispossessed.

Nevertheless the severe code of law under which the Forest had been placed, with its penalties of death, blinding or mutilation for poaching and lesser offences, caused bitter resentment among all classes. In Saxon law not even murder had been a capital offence, but was expiable by the payment of a fine in gold or cattle or by outlawry; and the idea that the life of a deer should outweigh that of a man was contrary to the common people's conception of justice. Nothing more is needed to explain why the arrow that took away the life of the hard Conqueror's harder son William Rufus as he hunted in Canterton Glen may neither have been an accident nor have come from the bow of Sir Walter Tyrell at all, but from that of some lowlier but more expert marksman of the subject race, lurking in the thickets. The Norman barons, too, hated this forest law which they regarded as another of the encroachments by which the Crown was building up the royal prerogative at their expense, and under which its officials could extort large sums from them without even a travesty of justice.

A step forward so far as the ordinary people of the Forest were concerned came in the thirteenth century when Henry III issued a charter laying down that in future no man should lose his life or limb for a poaching offence. He also abolished the barbarous custom of hamstringing dogs to prevent them from hunting and substituted the practice of 'lawing' or cutting off the claws of their forefeet, leaving them able to herd cattle but not to run down and kill the royal deer. In his reign, too, a shift of emphasis began between the importance of the venison (that is, the deer) and that of what was and still is called the 'vert' – to wit, the timber. Hitherto the protection of the deer had overridden everything else, but henceforward the vert was given increasing priority. At this time, too, the forest rights and customs presently to be described, which may have begun by way of minor concessions and easings of the law as compensation for the hardships it involved, were developing and becoming crystallized.

From the close of the Middle Ages onward the provision of timber from the Forest became of increasing importance; at first to ensure supplies of fuel and small stuff for charcoal-making, but afterwards more and more for shipbuilding. This led in stages to the enclosure by royal officials of areas in which the timber could be protected by the exclusion of the deer and the prohibition of pasturage. In 1698 an Act of Parliament provided for the immediate enclosure and planting with oaks of 2000 acres, followed by a further 4000 at the rate of 200 a year for 20 years. When these woods were safely established the enclosures were to be thrown open and another 6000 acres enclosed and planted in the same way. In actual fact only 3296 acres of the first option were taken up and the second option was not used; but the Act implied what was afterwards called the 'rolling power'; that is, that when a plantation had been safely nursed beyond the point of suffering harm from pastured stock and the fence had been thrown down to allow pasture to be resumed the Crown's officers were free to 'roll on', to enclose and plant up some other equivalent area. Should this ever be carried to the limit, it could result in the complete afforestation (in the modern sense of planting with trees) of the whole region, the disappearance of the open 'lawns' (as the more extensive glades of the New Forest are called) and heaths, and the consequent elimination or drastic reduction of feed for cattle and the foresters' common rights.

By an Act of 1808 the then existing enclosures were confirmed and further enclosures by the Office of Woods which had now come into existence were authorised up to a maximum of 6000 acres *at any one time* – words which still implied the rolling power. A further Act in 1851 gave powers to enclose another 10,000 acres in addition to these 6000 already provided for, and yet another 10,000 when the first 10,000 were thrown open after the trees on them were sufficiently grown. At the same time it was decided that since royal deer-hunts were a thing of the past and the feeding habits of deer were a danger to both timber and agriculture they should be exterminated. But though a drive was made for that purpose and thousands were destroyed, an estimated 2000 survived by taking refuge in the remoter recesses of the Forest. About 200 are still killed annually in deer drives, but nevertheless it is generally believed that this has done little or nothing more than keep pace with their natural increase, if even that.

As regards the rolling power and the commoners' consequent fears, tension was now mounting and new factors and interests had arisen. An influx had begun of upper- and upper-middle-class folk of education and means who were coming to live in the Forest and often acquiring commoners' rights thereby. Though not dependent on these rights as the native commoners were, they were people capable of leading campaigns in defence of them. Others, moreover, were now coming to the Forest for recreation or holidays and beginning to put forward a claim for the preservation of its facilities and amenities as a public playground.

By now there were three groups of Forest officials. The Lord Warden, who was the chief officer of the Forest, and his underlings supervised the deer and game and everything connected therewith. Four verderers, whose office had originated in the Middle Ages for the administration of the forest law whose shrunken remnant was now represented by the New Forest bye-laws, acted as quasi-justices chiefly concerned with such matters as encroachments on common land, the exercise of privileges of common by unqualified persons, thefts of heath, furze, fern or turves, and so forth. They were sworn to protect the Crown's rights in deer and timber from injury by the commoners in the exercise of their common rights and also to settle disputes between commoner and commoner over these, but were not meant to defend the commoners and their rights against the Crown and its officials. Thirdly there were the officers who, under the Office of Woods (which after its demise was reincarnated as the Forestry Commission in 1923), were responsible for the silvicultural management of the Forest; that is, for the enclosures, the growing of crops of timber in them, matters concerning the timber that remained on the open wastes, and the allocation of wood to comply with the rights of fuel. The head of these officers was the Deputy Surveyor of the Forest.

After 1851 and as a result of the putting down of the deer, the Lord

Wardenship became redundant and was allowed to lapse, the Deputy Surveyor becoming the chief officer of the Forest. Next, the outcome of the rising tension over the divergence and clash of interests was an Act of 1877 which has been called the Commoners' Charter. By this the rolling power was abolished, the commoners' rights were defined and protected, and the ancient Court of Verderers was reconstituted on an elective basis to be the guardian of these rights. As redefined and regularized by this Act they are as follows. The owners of certain smallholdings which may be no larger than five acres have the right to turn their cows, horses and geese out to pasture on the open wastes of what was once the king's forest but after the exchange of it and other forests for the annuities of the Civil List has become national property. There is also the 'common of mast', which is the right to turn pigs loose to forage for acorns and beech mast during the period of pannage from 25 September to the end of November, when the acorns are dropping. The 'common of estover', which is attached to houses and not persons, implies the right to take a specified quantity of wood from the Forest, provided that it is consumed in the house that carries the right; though anyone may take wood 'by hook or by crook', which means that they are entitled to any fallen wood that can be picked up without cutting. The right of turbary, which also pertains to houses, is the householder's right to cut turves for burning on his hearth. There are also the rights of digging marl for dressing the land and cutting bracken for bedding; and a right that has fallen into disuse since the conditions that produced it no longer exist is reflected in the presence on the map of an occasional 'purlieu', an area of land whose owner had leave to kill trespassing deer provided that they were slain before they re-entered the Forest.

The Act of 1877 increased the number of verderers to six, afterwards raised by an Act of 1949 to ten, of whom five are appointed and five elected. The present composition of the Verderers' Court is that an Official Verderer is appointed by the Crown and one representative each by the Ministry of Agriculture, the County Council Planning Authority, the Forestry Commission and the Countryside Commission. The remaining five are elected by the commoners for six years. To be eligible for election a verderer must occupy more than an acre of land to which the right of pasture is attached. The Court is served by three paid and five voluntary and unpaid agisters who ride the Forest to look after the welfare of the pastured animals and collect the fees which the commoners pay for the right to pasture them. They have been called the smallest police force in the world.

Besides the enforcement of the bye-laws a good part of the work of the Verderers' Court is now concerned with the ever-growing number of visitors, since both the verderers and the Forestry Commission have to ensure that the life and beauty of the Forest are not spoilt by this mounting pressure. The Court meets every second month in the Verderers' Hall of the Queen's House at Lyndhurst, which dates mainly from the seventeenth century though parts of it go back to Tudor times. It may impose fines, though there is a right of appeal from its decisions to the next Hampshire general or quarter sessions. In its courtroom hangs an ancient and gigantic stirrup which is said to have been used as a test of whether a Forest dog was large enough to be a danger to the deer. If it could not pass through the stirrup it was duly expedited or 'lawed' by the loss of the claws of its forefeet according to the custom afore-mentioned which had been introduced under Henry III. Though popularly known as King Rufus's Stirrup, this relic is thought to date only from the sixteenth century.

The total area within the 'Perambulation' or legal boundary of the Forest is 144 square miles. Within this area are many 'islands' of private freehold land which have been derived from the Crown in one way or another during the ages and now total up to a little more than one-third of the whole. The rest, about 101 square miles or 65,000 acres, remains under state ownership. Nearly all of this is available for the public's access and enjoyment, and can be divided into approximately 26,000 acres of woodland, 38,000 acres of open heath and 1000 acres of agricultural land and residential property. The 26,000 acres of woodland comprise 6000 classed as 'ancient and ornamental woods' (mainly beech and oak with a little natural Scotch pine) which the Act of 1949 had stipulated might be temporarily enclosed in order to ensure their regeneration but which remain open both to the public and the commoners' animals; 18,000 acres of the older statutory enclosures, of which 16,000 may be enclosed at any one time; and 2000 of a possible maximum of 5000 acres which the 1949 Act had also stipulated might be enclosed for silviculture. These two latter categories are fenced against the commoners' animals. Over the 38,000 acres of 'open forest' both the animals and the public are

19   Opposite above   *The ruins of the conjoint chapels of the Holy Ghost and Holy Trinity at Basingstoke.*

20   Opposite below   *Beaulieu Abbey: the former refectory, converted into the parish church.*

of course free to wander at large. The Forestry Commission is responsible for keeping these free from coarse vegetation and maintaining the 'passages' through the bogs and the necessary drainage. The balance of 1000 acres is represented by some plantations, a little agricultural land and many residences in which Forestry officials and staff live, all of which are Crown freehold.

At present perhaps 1800 ponies and 4000 cattle graze in the Forest, as well as the swine which feed in autumn on acorns and beech mast. The ponies, which may have been originally descended from the wild horses of ancient Britain, are still wild in the sense that they wander at will, but not in the sense of being ownerless, since they belong to commoners who for a nominal fee are entitled to graze them on the unenclosed parts of the Forest. The foals are branded at the annual autumn round-ups according to the brand of the mare with which they are running, and the horse foals not wanted for future stud purposes are sold at the Beaulieu Road Sale, while the branded fillies are turned back on the Forest with their mothers. About 1880 a controversial 'improvement' of the breed began. The original New Forest pony was a small, stocky, rather hairy and very hardy creature standing about eleven hands; the breed that provided pack ponies for rural transport and was much used by the local smugglers. But when people began to move into the Forest for retirement or part-time or full-time residence they set about 'improving' the breed by introducing Arab stallions. As a result the ponies became taller and lighter, but weaker; better-looking and thus more showy as saddle-ponies and in traps, but without the strength, toughness and placidity of the old stock.

Five species of deer are now found in the Forest, of which the red deer are the most uncommon and are rarely seen. The commonest are the fallow deer, estimated to number about 1000; and there are also an estimated 300 roe deer, who are mostly nocturnal and not often visible, as well as a few Japanese and Manchurian deer who have been introduced comparatively recently.

In addition there have been until very recently a few genuinely wild donkeys in the Forest. Those that remain, however, have been taken under the protection of humane individuals, since both they and many of the ponies were constantly stolen. This began on a small scale before the Second World War, but the pony population was then much larger than at present and the losses were almost negligible. With the war, however,

21   Opposite above *Langstone Harbour near Havant, at low tide: the comfortable and popular Royal Oak inn and the old mill, now transformed into a residence.*

22   Opposite below *Portsmouth: looking up the harbour past the Tower House towards Point, with dockyard buildings in the middle distance.*

came meat-rationing, and since the flesh of foals is almost indistinguishable from veal, gangs of raiders drove their vans into Forest bye-roads under cover of darkness, erected temporary stockades into which they herded unbranded foals, roped them and carried them off to slaughter-houses in spite of the efforts of police, forest officials and patrols of volunteers. When the motive for this large-scale poaching declined with the end of rationing, the increase of fast motor-traffic on the then unfenced main roads of the Forest replaced it as the greatest danger to the lives of the animals, which had been accustomed to wander freely on them, and this has now made it necessary to fence these roads in on both sides.

There are not so many oak trees in the Forest as might be expected; which is due not only to recent causes but to past heavy demands for the building of our navy's 'wooden walls' in earlier days. Nevertheless there are some mighty and ancient specimens: the Eagle Oak near where the road to Burley branches rightward from the A35 highway between Lyndhurst and Christchurch, its name allegedly deriving from an eagle being shot in its branches; the Knightwood Oak in the same inclosure (as the word is spelt in the Forest), which has a girth of over 17 feet; Peter's Oak in Holidays Inclosure not far away; and the King and Queen Oaks near Boldrewood Lodge a little further north. Almost opposite the Knightwood Inclosure on the other side of the main road the Mary Anderson Beech stands first among near-equals in Brinken Wood; in Marsh Ash Wood to the west of Holidays Inclosure there are several splendid beeches; near Fritham the giant Queen Beech stands on the edge of a plantation of her sisters; and there are more fine specimens in Anses Wood which fringes Fritham Plain on the south. Boldrewood Walk and Highland Water Inclosure further south again have some magnificent firs; and here and there in the Forest one comes upon aged yews.

The peril of heath and woodland fires in the dry season may be called the Forest's Public Menace Number One. A plantation that has taken from 60 to 120 years to mature can be destroyed in a few hours by a smouldering picnic fire or a cigarette carelessly tossed away; and indeed one fire that burnt out 200 acres of forest was traced to a match flicked through the window of a car. It is partly to avoid this danger that numerous gravelled car-parks, discreetly sited and of modestly unobtrusive size, have been provided.

The walks in the Forest are legion, though it is inadvisable to attempt them without a good map, and in an average season it is not till May that the lower parts become dry enough for any but the doughtiest walkers. Perhaps the finest (though personal familiarity may have led to bias here) is to be had by striking across Butts Lawn on the north side of Brockenhurst and then following upstream the winding course of Highland Water. The path leads through the intriguingly named Queen's Bower and a mile or two further on reaches the Lyndhurst-Christchurch road. Those who elect to cross this road and continue to follow the stream can go on to Highland Water Inclosure, through Puckpits and over Withybed Bottom to the Romsey-Ringwood road (A31) that is the other main artery through the Forest from north-east to south-west. Once it has passed Cadnam, where it enters the Forest, this is a lovely road – or it would be if it were not for the traffic; and even Cadnam has pleasant 'lawns' or glades and attractive woodland paths half-hidden behind its row of mean and ugly suburban houses and its rather too self-conscious but admittedly comfortable inn. From Cadnam the road climbs for a couple of miles through woodland and then runs for eight more along high ground and almost wholly through open country to Picket Post, soon after which the drop to Ringwood and the Avon valley begins. For most of these eight miles it skirts on its right hand the north-western part of the Forest, which is mainly relatively high with moorlands that are really wild; and it offers splendid views on both sides to those who can pull or step out of the stream of traffic sufficiently to enjoy them, especially south-eastward where the hills of the Isle of Wight close the distance, with fold upon fold of green and purple and golden forest in between.

From near Picket Post a lane on the right leads after a mile to Linford with its inclosure and brook and then into a little-known and comparatively unfrequented part of the Forest, where wild life in plenty can be seen, but where there are no villages of any size and only a few scattered farms. Here a succession of little streams run westward down to the Avon, and for the energetic walker perhaps the best of the many rambles to be had hereabouts can be obtained by taking a compass bearing due north and heading for Godshill on the Cadnam-Fordingbridge road eight miles away across these streams and their intervening ridges, without worrying too much about paths or tracks though a careful lookout should be kept for bogs to be detoured. There is also good walking north-eastward to the hamlet of Fritham, where there is a pleasant inn; and the road to Burley which takes off at Picket Post from the other or southern side of the A31 is another ridge-road for the first mile or so, from which there is a magnificent view over the Avon valley to the Dorset and Wiltshire downs. The finest version of this view, however, can be obtained by climbing a track on the right just before Burley Street is reached to the hill-fort on top of Castle Hill. The village of Burley itself is also a centre of excellent walks.

The capital of the New Forest is Lyndhurst, which was once an attractive village but has suffered somewhat through traffic. An almost continuous stream of vehicles, formed by the convergence at the top of the village of those from two main roads, pours through it during daylight. Its church is modern, but has an east window by Burne-Jones and a reredos with an idealised and yet realistic representation by Lord Leighton of the Wise and Foolish Virgins. In the churchyard lies Mrs Reginald Hargreaves, born Alice Liddell, a daughter of the Dean of Christ Church, Oxford, for whom his friend Charles Dodgson wrote *Alice in Wonderland* under the pen-name of Lewis Carroll.

Three miles north is Minstead, with a church about which opinions differ widely, for it is an amazing jumble of architectural styles. Perhaps its most striking features, however, are internal: a Norman font; a great seventeenth-century three-decker pulpit in whose lowest 'deck' the parish clerk used to sit and say his 'Amens' while the middle and top levels were used for the reading of the lessons and the preaching of the sermon respectively; and two enormous family pews, one with a fireplace, whose occupants must have been completely hidden from what they no doubt considered the vulgar curiosity of the rest of the congregation. In the churchyard Sir Arthur Conan Doyle the novelist and creator of Sherlock Holmes, in whose historical novel *The White Company* Minstead figures and who lived in the parish, is buried with his wife. On the village green the Trusty Servant inn has a signboard which can also be seen at Winchester College, of a man in eighteenth-century costume with a pig's head, a padlocked snout, an ass's ears, a stag's feet, a set of fire-irons in his hand and armed with sword and shield. Below it is a doggerel verse that runs:

A Trusty Servant's portrait would you see,

This emblematic Figure well survey,
The Porker's Snout not nice in diet shows
The Padlock shut no secret he'll disclose.
Patient the Ass his master's wrath will bear
Swiftness in errand the Stagg's feet declare;
Loaded his left hand apt to Labour saith:
The Vest his neatness, Open Hand his faith.
Girt with his Sword, his Shield upon his arm
Himself and Master he'll protect from harm.

A little further on and up a side-road are Furzey Gardens, well worth a visit; and not far away at Canterton on the other side of the A31 an unimpressive memorial known as the Rufus Stone but encased in an iron frame to protect it from vandals marks the spot where William Rufus met his mysterious end.

South-east of Lyndhurst is Beaulieu, aptly named, for it is – or was – a beautiful place, whose history has been written as a labour of love by the late Lord Montagu's former steward, Captain H. E. R. Widnell, in *The Beaulieu Record*. Here where one of the Forest streams broadens out into a tidal estuary King John, in an attempt to atone for his sins, founded an abbey that became one of the great Cistercian houses of the land, along with Fountains, Furness, Tintern, Rievaulx and Quarr. To it the Cistercians brought the sheep-husbandry which was a noted speciality of their order, aided by the fact that the terms of their grant gave them unlimited and free right of common of pasture for their sheep on the open wastes of the Forest. To this day these rights remain valid, inhering in every farm in Beaulieu and in others that are now parts of Brockenhurst or Boldre but were formerly included in the Abbey lands. The memory of this sheep-rearing is preserved in the still surviving name of one farm four miles south of Beaulieu on lighter and drier land more suitable for sheep than the river valley – Bergerie, which might be anglicised from its original Norman-French as Sheepcote. Other local names likewise reflect other aspects of the specialisation and division of labour of the Cistercians' farming: Beaufre Farm, less than a mile from the Abbey, where beeves were fatted, and Swinesley Farm to the west. At St Leonards near Bergerie there was an outlying grange with a chapel whose ruins remain, which served as a disciplinary unit where offending monks or lay brethren could be sent for a period of penitential hard labour; while at Sowley in the same area and Hatchet Mill a mile or so along the modern road to Brockenhurst the valleys of two forest brooks were dammed up by stout embanked causeways to create water-power for the production of iron. At both places the hammer ponds thus formed still remain.

At the Dissolution the Abbey passed like Titchfield's into the hands of Thomas Wriothesley, Earl of Southampton. The great fourteenth-century gatehouse became the new owner's dwelling and after the manor had passed through various hands was largely rebuilt in 1872 as Palace House. Much of the Abbey was pulled down and its stones were used to build Hurst Castle, another of Henry VIII's coastal defence forts, on a projecting spur of land at the western entrance to the Solent. The former refectory, however, has become the parish church, the lay brothers' dormitory a village hall, and the Domus below it a restaurant for visitors to the motor museum which the late Lord Montagu, an enthusiastic pioneer of motoring, established in Palace House and which his son has extended to its grounds. The cloisters also still survive, and the plan of the great Abbey church has been clearly marked out on the ground; but whereas it was formerly possible to visit the Abbey ruins separately and free of charge, a composite charge is now made which covers also (or primarily) a tour of Palace House and of the enormously expanded museum with its model railway, souvenir kiosks and restaurants. To accommodate the throngs of visitors who flock to these, huge coach and car parks have been carved out of the woods.

These hosts of people, pavilions and car parks must surely have driven away from Beaulieu the ghosts that have been alleged by many to haunt those buildings that date back to or are connected with the ancient Abbey. Various persons have claimed to have heard footsteps, both nocturnal and daylight, and other noises when nobody was visible or near enough to have made them; and some have asserted that they have seen apparitions. These phenomena have naturally been associated by those who have experienced them with the expulsion of the monks at the dissolution of the monasteries. It has even been said (and written) that after the stones from the buildings that were demolished then were used to build Hurst Castle the ghosts of displaced monks have been seen wandering there also, disconcerting among others some of the artillerymen who garrisoned the fort in more recent times. Even a battery-sergeant-major is reported to have maintained staunchly, when questioned sceptically by his commanding officer, that he had seen one, pointing out that as this had happened about breakfast-time he was stone-cold sober and since he was an Irishman and a Catholic he knew a Cistercian monk when he saw one.

A few miles further down the winding Beaulieu river is Bucklers Hard, a centre of shipbuilding 200 years ago and of yachting and yacht-building to-day. In the eighteenth century the second Duke of Montagu (a title which did not descend to the present Lords Montagu), who besides owning Beaulieu also owned sugar islands in the West Indies, hit upon the idea of making this into a port for trading with them. From the abbots of Beaulieu the river had inherited privileges as a free harbour, and there was of course ample timber for shipbuilding in the woods around. The project of developing a port for the sugar trade miscarried, but shipbuilding, mainly for warships, flourished at Bucklers Hard during the second half of the century, the most famous vessel built here being the *Agamemnon* which Nelson commanded during part of his earlier career. Early in the nineteenth century, however, the owners of the yard overreached themselves by entering into too-ambitious contracts which they failed to fulfil on time, and the yard collapsed; though besides the yacht-building which has developed in more modern times some sections of the Mulberry Harbour which facilitated the Allied landings on the Normandy coast during the Second World War were constructed here. The village, rather shrunken from what it once was, consists now of one broad street of cottages running downhill to the river. At the foot on the left is the eighteenth-century Master-Builder's House, now a hotel; and a room in a cottage just above it has been made into a memorial chapel to a young R.A.F. pilot who was killed in 1918 while flying over the Solent. More recently a maritime museum has been created just behind the top of the other side of the street.

Across the river from Bucklers Hard are the woods of Exbury, where from 1922 onwards Mr Lionel de Rothschild, whose business was banking but whose hobby was gardening on a colossal scale, converted the 600 acres of woodland he owned into 250 acres of garden and 350 of arboretum. His main love was rhododendrons, which are very easily cross-fertilised, and he obtained seeds and plants from all over the world, allowed the plants to cross-fertilise each other and grew the seedlings, scrapping every plant that yielded a flower which fell below his very high standard. The result is that in season the Exbury gardens, to which the public is admitted, carry a paradise of blossom.

South from Lyndhurst, along a road which runs through woodland scenery that is still striking in spite of the traffic, is Brockenhurst, a large residential village just outside which on a wooden hill further to the south stands a church that claims to be the oldest in the Forest. An earlier church almost certainly existed here, since the Norman builders of the present one incorporated some of its walling in their work. A mighty yew in the churchyard has a girth of more than 20 feet at five feet from the ground. North of the village are Butts Lawn and Balmer Lawn, two of the largest lawns in the Forest, the former of which almost certainly owes its name, not to bygone archery practice as some have thought, but to the 'butts' or headlands of flatter ground that cross the ends of the ridge-and-furrow pattern still to be seen on it, showing where the plough teams of eight oxen apiece must have been repeatedly turned centuries ago.

Not far west of Brockenhurst is Sway, near which is a 'folly' known as Peterson's Tower that is a landmark for miles around. 218 feet high, it was built about a hundred years ago of concrete, then a very unusual building material, by Andrew Peterson, an eccentric who had retired from a judgeship in India. He left instructions that he should be buried under it and thereafter a strong light should be kept burning at the top of it as an inland beacon for shipping in the Solent; but the authorities decided that the lamp would be more likely to confuse than help navigation, and forebade both the light and the burial. Peterson, who had also wished to show the constructional virtues of concrete, had likewise built two other towers and several farm and other buildings of it.

A mile or so seawards from Peterson's Tower is the village of Hordle, where in the late nineteenth century a community of the eccentric American religious sect known as the Shakers existed for a time. Originally an early eighteenth-century offshoot from the English Quakers, called 'the Shaking Quakers' from their ecstatic movements during their services, they migrated to America in 1774 and in due course established a number of communities there. This backthrust Hordle branch at first attained some notoriety, and brakeloads of people would drive over from Southampton on Sundays to watch their antics, but after the death of their 'prophetess' Mrs Girling they became extinct, as they now virtually are in the United States.

South of Brockenhurst Highland Water becomes the Boldre River and then the Lymington River. The little village of Boldre has a church that is a harmonious mixture of the Norman and Early English styles, and here William Gilpin, the author of *Forest Scenery* and the most influential of all writers on picturesque travelling, who has been called the Gilbert White of the New Forest, ministered from 1777 to his death in 1804. It was in Boldre church that the poet Southey married his second wife Caroline Bowles, who had lived till the age of 53 in a cottage at Buckland near Lymington. Thirty years previously she had sent one of her poems to Southey, who encouraged her so much that they formed a sort of literary partnership that came to nothing in itself but led to a steady correspondence. When Southey's first wife's mind gave way and she died insane he wrote to Caroline, after a decent interval, proposing marriage and on her accepting him he came south from Keswick for the ceremony. By now he was 65, however, and three months later his own mental powers failed; and when he died after three unhappy years Caroline returned to Buckland. Just inside Boldre church door, too, there is a memorial to Admiral Holland and the 1416 officers and men of the battle-cruiser *Hood* which was sunk by the German battleship *Bismarck* in the last war.

Lymington, the largest and most attractive town in the region, is officially outside the Forest, but very much in and of it in practice, for here the people of all the neighbouring parts of it come to do their shopping. In the Middle Ages it was a port of some consequence and even something of a rival to Southampton. The latter's port then stretched officially from Langstone Harbour beyond Portsmouth on the east to Hurst Castle on the west and therefore included Lymington, whose inhabitants nevertheless disputed hotly the claim of Southampton officials to collect customs duties there. Even an agreement of 1334 by which Southampton leased its rights to Lymington for £30 did not end the quarrel, especially since a practice seems to have developed of Southampton shippers who wanted to avoid their own town's heavier dues landing their goods at Lymington Quay instead. It was on the manufacture and export of salt from the neighbouring saltearns, however, that the town's prosperity depended; but this was injured by taxation in the eighteenth century and collapsed finally after the 1860s in the face of the competition of mined salt from Cheshire exported from Liverpool. Smuggling was also an activity encouraged by the abundance of creeks and by the inhabitants, and when it declined the growth of yachting in the later nineteenth century began the port's development into a major sailing centre second on the Hampshire mainland only to Hamble in the Solent. To-day the town on a Saturday night is (as Mr Brian Vesey Fitzgerald has written) a mixture of market town, seaport and fair. On a less busy day the best way to see it is to come from Boldre down the far bank of the river, cross it by the former toll-bridge, walk up Quay Hill with its pavement of setts and its cheerful bay-windowed cottages, and then up the wide main street with its mixture of architecture varying from the seventeenth to the twentieth century as far as the handsome church at the top of the hill. Looking back from here across the river one sees among the trees of the farther bank an obelisk that commemorates Admiral Sir Harry Burrard Neale, whose family the Burrards – he had taken his wife's surname of Neale after marriage – lived for many generations at Walhampton House nearby, which is now a school. Another member of the family, General Sir Harry Burrard, earned an unfortunate notoriety at the beginning of the Peninsular War as one of the two senior generals who took over from Lieutenant-General Sir Arthur Wellesley, afterwards the Duke of Wellington, on the morrow of his first brilliant victory at Vimiero and threw away most of its fruits, after which they were never employed on active service again.

Along the coast to the westward there are two or three 'residential' seaside villages of which Milford-on-Sea with a church that is well worth visiting is the pleasantest and has kept most character, in the centre at least. Nearby is the gravelly spit that runs out to Hurst Castle; and a few miles further on is the county's new boundary, for Highcliffe, Christchurch and Bournemouth have been cast into Dorset by the recent rearrangement of local government, and Hampshire has thus been deprived of both Christchurch Priory and the mouth of the river Avon, though much of the middle and lower course remains to it.

Ringwood, past which the river flows higher up its course, is not a town of much interest, though it has an attractive manor-house and in its High Street there is another house in which the unhappy Duke of Monmouth, brought there as a captive after the defeat of his rebellion at Sedgemoor, is said to have written his futile and craven appeal for mercy to his uncle James II. Nor does Fordingbridge at the north-west corner of the Forest (though like Lymington it is technically outside it) merit much comment. Its best building is its sturdy church, mostly 700 years old; and in a pleasant public park beside the river at the southern entrance to the town there is a rather infelicitious statue of the painter Augustus John. Between the two places is Ellingham church, which has no village and is where Dame Alice Lisle was buried, who at the age of 71 was sentenced by the unspeakable Judge Jeffries to be burnt to death for sheltering two fugitives from Monmouth's army in her home at Moyles Court, a mid-seventeenth-century brick house nearby. The sentence was commuted by James II to death by beheading.

North of Fordingbridge is Breamore, whose church is by far the most important and interesting Saxon survival in the county, and dates from about 1000. In its porch there is a monumental rood in relief, with figures of Our Lady and St John, which has been mutilated by some miscreant but must originally have been a striking sculpture. Breamore House, a late Elizabethan brick-built mansion which lost much of its architectural interest when it was rebuilt after a mid-Victorian fire, stands a few hundred yards north of the church. For well over 200 years it has been the seat of the Hulse family, who have gathered in that time a remarkable collection of works of art. On the down above it, in the heart of a little wood, there is another mysterious earthwork maze like that on St Catherine's Hill near Winchester. Just across the river from Breamore are the largely eighteenth-century church and manor-house of Hale, both of them mainly the work of Thomas Archer, a highly individual architect who redesigned the house for himself about 1715, though another hand remodelled it again 50 years later.

To the west of Fordingbridge and Breamore a small salient of Hampshire, which has been called the Martin peninsula after the pretty village of that name which occupies its apex, thrusts itself briefly between Wiltshire and Dorset. One result of this is to incorporate a short stretch of Grim's Ditch in the county boundary hereabouts. This earthwork, thought by some to have been a defensive fosse and by others the boundary of a large Bronze Age cattle ranch, was popularly supposed in the distant and superstitious past to have been built by the devil, for whom Grim was a synonym or prudent euphemism used by those who feared to rouse his anger by naming him more bluntly. The Martin salient also includes Rockbourne, which has one of the prettiest village streets in Hampshire and near which a Roman villa, the first clue to whose former existence here was discovered in 1942 by a farmer while digging out a ferret, has recently been excavated and is open to public view. In the neighbourhood also there are two notable barrows, one of which, called Knap, is the largest in the county, while the other, strangely named Duck's Nest, is one of the finest in it. Near the village, too, on a hill in the former grounds of West Park, a now demolished house where his family once lived, there is a column erected in memory of General Sir Eyre Coote, a contemporary of Robert Clive who by his victories over both the French and hostile native powers did almost as much as he to lay the foundations of our empire in India.

TEN

The Isle of Wight

In a sense, Queen Victoria can be said to have discovered the Isle of Wight. Before she made Osborne House her seaside home in the 1840s the island was left pretty much to itself, apart from the development of Cowes as a yachting centre that had begun about thirty years earlier. But after the Queen's advent more and more people followed her example and came to it for holidays and some of them, like Tennyson, to live there and enjoy its quiet beauty, so that she brought great prosperity to what came to be known as the Garden of England. For a long time it continued to deserve that title, but now that for two-thirds of the year fleets of huge coaches filled with sightseers follow one another along the roads it can be more fitly described as one of the country's playgrounds. This nevertheless means that it gives pleasure to a great many more people than before, and the tourist trade provides the main revenue by which it lives.

The island is small, 23 miles at most from east to west and a maximum of 15 from north to south. There are three main crossings from the mainland, to its east, centre and west respectively: from Portsmouth to Ryde, with a supplementary car ferry from Portsmouth to Fishbourne; from Southampton to Cowes; and from Lymington to Yarmouth; both of which last two are made by car ferries. The crossings from Portsmouth and Southampton can now also be made quickly by hovercraft; but for those who prefer a minimum of crowds and seek such solitude as can still be obtained it is best − given a taste and aptitude for walking − to take the Lymington-Yarmouth route and after exploring Yarmouth cross either on foot or by a short bus-ride to Freshwater Bay, setting out afterwards along the ridge of downs that forms the island's spine and offers splendid views on either side.

The Wight was not always an island, but was joined to the mainland until well after the last Ice Age and perhaps much later. Before its separation, what historical geographers have called the Solent river (a southern counterpart of the Thames whose upper course is represented to-day by the Dorset Frome) flowed eastward to fall into a Channel that was much narrower then than now. From the north this river received as tributaries the ancestors of the Avon, Southampton Water and the Meon among others; and from the south those of the Medina and the other and lesser streams of the present island. To the south of this river system ran a then continuous chalk barrier of which the Purbeck downs and the spinal ridge of the Isle of Wight survive as sections that are now separated by a gap of nearly 20 miles, though with the Old Harry Rocks and the Needles as their respective outlying fragments. When in post-glacial times the relatively rapid rise of the sea-level forced this gap through the chalk barrier the valley of the middle and lower Solent river was flooded and the Isle of Wight was thus separated from the mainland. This was accompanied by the drowning of the lower courses of the affluents of the Solent, creating those wide estuaries which, where they have been preserved by natural tidal scour, have already been commented upon as a characteristic of Hampshire rivers.

The river Medina, which almost divides the island in two, since it rises among the downs just behind its southern apex and then flows north through a gap in the main chalk ridge to the Solent at Cowes, shares this characteristic. There are two other rivers, which curiously enough are both named Yar. The West Yar, like the Medina, rises close to the island's south coast and flows north to fall into the Solent at Yarmouth, practically severing the western end of the island from the remainder; but the East Yar, rising south of the main ridge, flows north-eastward into Bembridge harbour just about where the Solent merges into the Channel. South of its source and the Medina's, there is a second mass of chalk downs, whose southern escarpment falls to the magnificent line of cliffs that here fringe the island's coast and form a contrast to the low wooded hills of much of its northern shore.

The Romans, who seized the island very early in their occupation of Britain, built a fortress where Carisbrooke Castle now stands; and in due course Romano-British villas arose of which the remains of one at

Brading are among the finest in the country. After their departure the island was settled by Jutes, who were later conquered by the West Saxons and absorbed into the kingdom of Wessex; though during the eleventh century it was occupied by the Danes as a base for harrying the Saxon coast. In the Middle Ages it was several times raided by the French, and in a particularly disastrous raid in 1377 Newport, Yarmouth and Ryde were burnt. Under Henry VIII's scheme of coastal defence forts equipped with cannon were built at Yarmouth, Sandown and East and West Cowes on both sides of the Medina, to match the construction of Hurst, Calshot and Southsea Castles on the mainland opposite; and since a very formidable attack by a large French force in 1545 no enemy has set foot on the island. Nor did it see fighting during the Civil War, since it was controlled by the Parliamentarians, whom most of the islanders supported, though the gentry were mainly Royalists. At this time the roads were still only rutted tracks and nearly all travel was on foot or horseback, with ladies riding pillion and goods carried by packhorses. Even in the eighteenth century the island remained a remote place; in 1770 there was only one vehicle obtainable for hire in the whole of it, and as late as 1792 only one postmaster and one postman. A good deal of ploughing was still done by oxen, and tradesmen's carts were in some parts drawn by dogs; while smuggling flourished on a grand scale until well on in the nineteenth century and may almost be considered one of the island's main industries until then, along with fishing, agriculture, quarrying, shipbuilding and lace-making, before catering for holiday-makers and tourists came to the fore.

Except Newport in the centre, all the island's towns are situated on the coast. Those which have developed as resorts have pleasant seaside terraces with period balconies and ornate pilasters, stucco fronts and external verandahs climbing up among the conifers, above the lawns and awnings of the sea-fronts. These were the island's version of the great outburst of building development and improvement that took place all over England after Victoria's accession. On the other hand the old parts of Yarmouth and Cowes (in spite of the latter's considerable industrialization) have kept a definite flavour of antiquity, and Newport has many old houses. But it is to the villages and manor-houses, many of the latter Elizabethan and some of the smaller ones even older, that one must look for the real architectural charm of the island. Good building

stone was abundant and the cottages built of it naturally resemble those of
neighbouring Dorset; while almost every village can show a church that is
at least interesting, even if none has the beauty and distinction that can be
found in Somerset or East Anglia.

The island's most beautiful feature, however, is its coastline, which can
best be seen (though certainly not in solitude) by taking the
round-the-island boat trip operated from Ryde, which is a popular seaside
town with miles of beach and half-a-mile of pier that is nevertheless not
dedicated to amusements but necessitated by the very gradual shelving of
the sands that prevents vessels of any depth of draught from coming
nearer the shore. Near it on the east is the smaller resort of Seaview,
which also has a good beach of gently-sloping firm sand and therefore
plenty of shallow-water bathing and paddling suitable for small children;
and a couple of miles west of it is Quarr Abbey, old and new. Little
remains of the original Cistercian monastery founded in the twelfth
century; but early in the 1900s some French Benedictine monks from the
great abbey of Solesmes in Normandy bought a nearby house with its
grounds, in which they built a striking modern abbey designed by one of
themselves, Dom Paul Bellot, a pioneer of twentieth-century
Expressionism. Though he also designed many buildings in France,
Holland, Belgium and Canada, Quarr – of which he remained a monk –
was his outstanding achievement.

Close to Quarr are Fishbourne, where the car ferry from Portsmouth
lands, and Wootton Creek, an attractive tidal inlet with well-wooded
shores. Between this and East Cowes is Osborne, on the site of an earlier
large eighteenth-century house. As a princess Victoria had twice visited
the island with her mother the Duchess of Kent, and after she came to the
throne and married Prince Albert the royal couple wanted a private house,
'quiet and retired', as she wrote to her uncle King Leopold of Belgium.
They therefore bought the Osborne estate in 1845, had the old house
pulled down and substituted another in an Italianate style which Prince
Albert, who had a measure of artistic talent, designed himself; though he
employed Thomas Cubitt, who built many of the London squares and
terraces of this period, as builder and probably to some extent as architect
also. The royal family used to come here regularly twice a year; from
mid-July to mid-August in order to include the Cowes Regatta Week, and
from mid-December to mid-February so that they could spend Christmas

23   Opposite   *A quiet corner on the Beaulieu river.*

there; in addition to which the Queen used to seize every chance of a few days' rest and quiet there at other times. After her death her son Edward VII gave the house, which had been her private property, to the nation; and the Royal Naval College was established in the grounds until it was removed to Dartmouth after the First World War. To-day the house, with its lofty apartments crammed with furniture, ornaments, curios, china, bric-à-brac, pictures and sculpture, is a memorial to the Queen, though part of it is also a convalescent home for officers and the beautiful grounds are a sanctuary for birds.

East Cowes, which is partly residential and partly industrial, has another major house of some note: Norris Castle, built by James Wyatt in 1799 as a romantic reproduction or imitation of a Norman castle. It is a striking sight from the sea, with its lawn plunging straight down to the water.

Yacht-racing began at Cowes in the second half of the eighteenth century, though yachting was first heard of in the days of Charles II. The first regatta (a word which comes from the name given at Venice to certain boat-races held on the Grand Canal) was apparently held in 1776, though only naval vessels seem to have taken part in it. When after Trafalgar Britain was indisputably mistress of the seas, however, and it was no longer necessary for fleets of merchantmen to accumulate in Cowes Roads waiting for warships to convoy them to their various destinations, Cowes began to blossom as a pleasure resort. Private yacht-racing began to take place about 1810, though often between two yachts only, with heavy bets on the results. In 1815 the Yacht Club was founded, and racing on any considerable scale really dates from this time. In 1817 the Prince Regent joined the Club, which became 'Royal' when he became King George IV in 1820. Its uniform of 'a common blue jacket, with white trousers', adopted a few years later, was described as 'far from unbecoming to such as are not too square in the stern'. George IV's brother and successor William IV changed the name to Royal Yacht Squadron, and in 1858 it acquired as its headquarters the old West Cowes Castle, which had originally been one of Henry VIII's coastal forts. Queen Victoria's son and heir Edward, Prince of Wales, took a great interest in yachting and when he joined the Squadron and became commodore a few years later his presence and influence caused Cowes Week to become increasingly fashionable, so that £70 a week (a

24 Opposite above *The lovely Mottisfont Abbey, a one-time monastery converted successively into a Tudor house and then into an eighteenth-century mansion.*

25 Opposite below *The village street of Selborne, with Gilbert White's house, The Wakes, towards the end on the left.*

considerable sum then) is said to have been paid by visitors for two small sitting-rooms and bedrooms. George V and the Duke of Edinburgh afterwards kept up the succession of royal yachtsmen, though yachting has not of course been confined to the upper strata of society, and many other sailing clubs, some of them more democratic, grew up in the island.

A few miles westward along the coast from Cowes are the scanty remains of Newtown on the shore of another tidal inlet. As its name implies, this was a made town and not one which grew naturally. Like New Alresford and some others, it owed its origin to a bishop of Winchester, being founded in 1256 by Bishop Aymer. Though burnt by the French in 1377, it was rebuilt and continued to have some importance as a port on the Solent, having (it was boasted) anchorage for 50 ships in the days of its prosperity, and a busy market where the green is now. But the harbour gradually silted up and the town declined, though it continued to return two members to Parliament until the Reform Bill of 1832, well before which time it had become one of the more notorious 'rotten boroughs'. To-day it consists, apart from a nineteenth-century church built in thirteenth-century style, only some Georgian cottages and a little town hall, now in the care of the National Trust, which stands isolated from any other building; though the line of the two parallel thirteenth-century streets can still be traced.

Yarmouth, a few miles further westward, was the most important town in the island in the earlier Middle Ages, but afterwards it declined until about 1800 it had fewer than a hundred inhabitants. Subsequently it grew again gradually, but the two members it had returned to Parliament since the days of Elizabeth I were taken away from it by the Reform Bill and it ceased to be a municipal borough in 1891. Latterly it has developed as a minor yachting and boat-building centre and has also profited from the influx of tourists through it to the western end of the island, but it is still a small place. The castle which Henry VIII built, though it continued to be garrisoned till the 1870s, is now dismantled and in the grounds of an hotel; while the apparent gunports in the wall of a house called 'The Towers' to the east of the town are merely painted imitations provided in the early eighteenth century to deceive the French by a naval captain who lived in the house. In the seventeenth-century church there is a monument on the tomb of Sir Robert Holmes, who was governor of the island in the days of Charles II and one of his most distinguished admirals, which purports to be a statue of Sir Robert. It was however originally meant to represent Louis XIV. Finished except for the head, it was being taken by sea to France to have this carved from life when the admiral captured it and decided to have his own head copied and put on it so that it could serve to adorn his tomb. The George Hotel near the Castle was formerly his house and though much modernised still contains a seventeenth-century staircase and panelling.

It was at Yarmouth that the painter George Morland stayed in 1799 in an attempt to escape his creditors. A master of genre and animal painting, he is estimated to have produced 4000 pictures, the best known and most characteristic of which were faithful reflections of lowly life in the England of that day. For about 15 years before his death in a sponging-house in 1804 at the age of 41 he lived at various places in the island, fraternising with countryfolk and fishermen, smugglers and poachers, from whom he drew many of his subjects, and indulging the taste for dissipation which he had developed early in life. For a time, accompanied by a faithful valet whose task it was to ward off duns, he tried to hide from his creditors at Cowes, where he had a patron, and it was when his retreat there was discovered that he moved on to Yarmouth. Here, however, he was arrested as a spy – it being a period of war with France when invasion was much feared – and when he produced some of his paintings to prove his innocence they were suspected in the excited atmosphere of the day of being disguised plans intended to help the French. In particular, one picture of a spaniel was actually thought to be a camouflaged map of the island. In justice it might be said that during the eighteenth century a number of very genuine spies, some of them Englishmen in French pay, had operated with varying success along the coasts of Hampshire and other parts of southern England. During the previous war with France a very daring and able French officer disguised himself as a British seaman – probably passing as a Channel Islander, which would have accounted then for something of a French accent – and, after penetrating Portsmouth, inspecting its fortifications, and surveying the Channel Fleet at Spithead from a boat, landed in the island and toured part of its interior, before getting clear away. The unhappy Morland was duly marched under military escort to Newport, where he was hooted by a mob as he was conveyed through the streets. The Bench, however, acquitted him of espionage after the landlord of the George at Yarmouth had given evidence on his behalf, and dismissed him with a caution.

Further west again and beyond Yarmouth are the small modern holiday resort of Totland Bay and then the coloured cliffs of Alum Bay. These cliffs, one of the island's natural wonders, are due to some great convulsion which at a remote period caused the various strata to be upheaved so that the layers with their different colours are perpendicular instead of horizontal. From Alum Bay there is a comparatively close view of the famous Needles, though a better one can be obtained in the summer by taking one of the boat trips which are operated locally.

Some miles inland up the river Medina that divides East and West Cowes and almost splits the island in two, is its capital, Newport, which has an old grammar school dating from 1619 and some seventeenth-century and Georgian houses. Nearby is Carisbrooke Castle, built in Norman times and still retaining its Norman keep and part of the Norman curtain wall but strengthened with bastions by an Italian military engineer in Queen Elizabeth's later years. It was here that after the Civil War Charles I, having briefly escaped from the captivity in which he had been held by Parliament, sought refuge under the mistaken impression that Colonel Hammond, the Parliamentarian governor of the castle, would help him to get away to France. Hammond, however, remained loyal to Parliament and held him prisoner, though Charles made more than one unsuccessful attempt to escape again. After his execution his two youngest children, Princess Elizabeth and Henry Duke of Gloucester, were interned at Carisbrooke by Parliament. The Princess died of a fever within a month, but Henry was eventually released and allowed to go abroad.

A more modern prison is that at Parkhurst, just to the north, which was opened in 1838 in buildings taken over from a pre-existing military hospital. In 1966 the new Albany model prison was established here.

The best of the inland villages of the island is probably Godshill a few miles west of Shanklin, even though it has paid the penalty of its attractiveness and its main-road position by becoming a rather too self-conscious show-place; not without some excuse, it may be said at once, for its thatched and stone-built cottages cluster delightfully around the mainly fifteenth-century church to which its wooded lanes lead. North of it is Arreton with a Jacobean manor-house and a church that combines every architectural style from Saxon (its tower has the oldest Saxon work in the island) to Perpendicular. Merstone Manor a mile to the south-west is a Jacobean brick-built house of a deep red colour; and away on the other side of the gap where the Medina cuts through the island's central downland spine is Gatcombe where again, as at Arreton, church and manor-house stand close together under the steep slope of a down. The church has various interesting features and the house, built in 1750 and formerly the seat of the Worsleys, is now National Trust property. A few miles westward over the downs is Calbourne with a village green, a group of great elms, some charming cottages and a still mainly thirteenth-century church. The best of these cottages, standing in a row along Winkle Street on the bank of the Caul Bourne, are rather hidden away and sometimes overlooked by the superficial and over-hasty visitor. Swainstone House to the north-east is mainly eighteenth-century, but has attached to it a thirteenth-century chapel and hall dating from the days when the manor was held by the bishops of Winchester, which fortunately escaped intact when the house was burnt out during a German air-raid in 1941. At Shalfleet nearby the miracle of the saving of Winchester Cathedral was repeated on a small scale, for when the church tower, the oldest in the island, was found to be standing in ten feet of clay and water its foundations were relaid in concrete and it was saved.

The least-visited part of the Isle of Wight is that which is called 'The Back of the Island' or 'The Back of the Wight' — the south-western coastal region between the Needles and St Catherine's Point. But though this lacks the grandeur of the south-east coast on the other side of the Point, it enjoys on the whole a comparative peace that together with its bracing air, attractive villages and lovely old manor-houses gives it a quiet charm. Freshwater Bay, its one little resort, is probably the least spoilt in the island; though at the other end of this stretch of the coast coaches and visitors flock to Blackgang Chine, an impressive and precipitous ravine which is said to derive its name from a notorious band of smugglers who at one time used it as a convenient way up from the shore.

Near Freshwater Bay in the 1860s and 1870s lived a remarkable women, Mrs Julia Cameron, who was one of the pioneers of photographic portraiture. Born in India, where she married a distinguished lawyer and where both of them took a great interest in native welfare, she came to England with him in 1848. Here they became noted for their humanitarianism and generosity and about 1865, having been given a camera by her family, she developed a great interest in photography, converting her coal-cellar into a darkroom and a henhouse into a studio, and conscripting or cajoling friends, neighbours, villagers and visitors into submitting to what was then the rather lengthy process of having their pictures taken. Since the Camerons were people of some note, these visitors who were persuaded to pose included such celebrities as Darwin, Browning and Tennyson. It was indeed Tennyson's residence near Freshwater and friendship with them which had been a main motive for their coming to live there, though this friendship did not prevent him from complaining that one of Mrs Cameron's photographs of him had made him 'look like a dirty monk'. Another notable friend and neighbour was Dr Jowett the famous Master of Balliol College, Oxford, for whom Mrs Cameron with her almost embarrassing generosity built a cottage to enable him to work in peace and seclusion on his translation of Plato.

It was at Farringford near Freshwater village (as distinct from Freshwater Bay), an eighteenth-century house in Strawberry Hill Gothic style which Tennyson bought soon after he became poet laureate, that he lived continuously from 1853 to 1867, and at intervals during the rest of his life. Of it he wrote:

> *. . . Far from the noise of smoke and town*
> *I watch the twilight falling brown*
> *All round a careless-ordered garden*
> *Close to the ridge of a noble down,*
> *For groves of pine on either hand*
> *To break the blast of winter stand*
> *And further on, the hoary channel*
> *Tumbles a billow on chalk and sand.*

The monument on his 'noble down', now called Tennyson Down and overlooking the house, marks his favourite walk, where he used to stride along in his cloak and his big broad-brimmed black hat of which the locals used to say that once round it was twice round Freshwater, breathing the air that he declared was worth sixpence a pint. But as he grew in fame he became increasingly embarrassed by people who were anxious to catch a sight of him, and retired to an estate at Aldworth near

Haslemere in Surrey, where he died. Farringford is now a hotel, but has been kept much as it was in Tennyson's time, and in the grounds is a Wellingtonia tree allegedly planted by Garibaldi when he visited the poet there.

The whole southern side of the island was a hotbed of smuggling until well into the nineteenth century. The entire population, squires and parsons often included, would combine to outwit the revenue officers and the trade was extremely well organised. Small boats that were difficult to detect ran across from France, many of them with false bottoms in which kegs of brandy were stowed that were either sunk at some spot convenient for collecting them when the coast was clear, or run ashore at night and hidden in caves or thickets near the beach. After collection they were stored in such hiding-places as farmhouse cellars or even the old-fashioned box-like tombstones in churchyards. One favourite ruse was to disguise contraband goods as, or underneath, yachts' washing being conveyed to the shore, which gave a special meaning to the innocent-seeming enquiry 'Has the washing come yet?' which could be heard on these occasions.

The westernmost of the villages near the coast at 'the Back of the Wight', Brook, is rather undistinguished; but then comes Mottistone with a charming manor-house that was originally Tudor and was so tactfully restored in the 1920s that its attractiveness has if anything been enhanced. On the hillside above the village and accessible by a path that begins at a gate opposite the church is the Long Stone, the island's only megalithic monument; and close by is a much overgrown earthwork on Castle Hill, from which there is a fine view along the coast. A mile or two eastward is Brighstone, a pleasant village partly marred by some modern eyesores; and a couple of miles further on lies Shorwell, perhaps the most attractive village in the island, rich in lovely cottages and with a chiefly Perpendicular church that contains a fifteenth-century painting depicting the legend of St Christopher. It is handsomely situated in a combe below the downs; and very close at hand are three of the island's finest Elizabethan and Jacobean houses: North Court, dating from 1615, where the poet Swinburne, who was born and partly brought up at Bonchurch a few miles away, lost his heart temporarily in his youth to Mary Gordon the daugher of the house; West Court, begun under Henry VIII but mainly Elizabethan with some Jacobean extensions; and

Wolverton Manor with a very fine Elizabethan front. Two miles further along the road to Chale is Kingston, with a comely but relatively undistinguished Jacobean manor-house; and near it Billingham Manor, a very fine and mainly early Georgian house embodying part of a Jacobean predecessor. During the early part of Charles I's imprisonment at Carisbrooke he was allowed to visit there, and there is a legend that his ghost haunts the present house.

Just beyond Chale the downs rise to the second highest point in the island, St Catherine's Hill (780 feet), commanding wide views westward over Chale Bay and crowned by the remains of two old lighthouses. For centuries the bay with its cruel cliffs was a menace to shipping, and in the fourteenth century the lighthouse whose shell still survives near the south end of the down was built, with a now vanished oratory where a priest could say masses for the souls of those who perished at sea. Until the dissolution of the monasteries and chantries in the sixteenth century the light was maintained, but since the oratory was counted as a chantry it was then suppressed and the light with it, though the tower was allowed to remain as a seamark. Then in 1785 a circular lighthouse whose stump still stands was begun nearby but not completed since it was found that it stood too high for the light to be seen in foggy weather. The two lighthouses are popularly known as 'the Mustard-Pot' and 'the Pepper-Box' respectively. Finally the present lighthouse was built on the beach at St Catherine's Point and first lighted in 1840, though even this did not prevent occasional wrecks later. On the down there is also a monument erected by Michael Hoy, a British merchant who had lived many happy years in Russia, to commemorate the Tsar Alexander I's visit to Britain after Napoleon's first downfall in 1814. Rather incongruously a second inscription was added after the Crimean War in commemoration of that conflict, in which the two former allies of 1814 fought each other.

Along the coast between St Catherine's Point and Dunnose beyond Ventnor there is a magnificent line of jagged cliffs forming what has been called perhaps the most remarkable stretch of coastline in England. The brown greensand rock of these, overhanging the soft and unstable gault or 'blue slipper' below, began at some remote period to form a series of landslips that have produced a double line of cliffs, with a sheltered dip running along between them. Known as the Undercliff, this dip is in part a tumbled mass of rocks and trees and bushes where tropical flowers may be found. Halfway along the beautifully wooded road that leads through it from the pleasant village of Niton the steep and therefore inappropriately-named Cripples' Path up the cliff leads shortly to Whitwell, which has an interesting church with a chapel to the Virgin Mary dating from about 1200 that was once a shrine to which pilgrims came. Two or three miles away across the downs and beautifully situated in wooded country, is Appledurcombe, once the grandest of all the island's houses and Hampshire's masterpiece of English Baroque. It was built in the first decade of the eighteenth century on the site of an Elizabethan predecessor by Sir Robert Worsley, whose family had been prominent in the island for the previous 200 years and who is commemorated by an obelisk on the hill above, from which there is a magnificent view over almost the whole interior of the island. After the Worsley family died out in the nineteenth century the house became first a school and then a place of refuge for those same Benedictine monks expelled from Solesmes who later migrated to Quarr. In 1943 a landmine which was dropped near it damaged it so badly that it has been abandoned as a ruin.

Ventnor, which before 1841 was only a small hamlet in the parish of its neighbour Bonchurch, owes its reputation as a winter resort partly to the shelter given it by the cliffs behind and partly to a medical treatise published in that year by Sir James Clarke, an eminent doctor of the day. In it he drew attention to its mild climate and wrote of the Undercliff that it bade fair to excel all other winter residences in the country. The slopes on which the town is built, however, are so steep that the terraces rise one above another on the edges of zigzag roads with corkscrew turns. Above them again is the still more precipitous Boniface Down, which at 787 feet is the highest point in the island. It is presumably because of its height that, though National Trust property, it is crowned by the pylons of a radar station.

Bonchurch, Ventnor's parent, is an old village with two churches, ancient and modern, both dedicated to St Boniface. In the churchyard of the modern church the poet Swinburne and the novelist H. de Vere Stacpoole, who lived here, are buried; and from Monks' Bay just below the village there is a delightful four-mile walk to Shanklin by way of the wooded headland of Dunnose and then past Luccombe Chine, a pretty ravine, to the picturesque and better-known Shanklin Chine. At the top of the latter is the village of Old Shanklin, and not far away there is the cliff-top walk known as Keats Green from the fact that the poet once lived here, as he also did at Newport, in the unavailing hope of curing the consumption from which he afterwards died in Italy. It was not till 30 years later, in the middle of the nineteenth century, that the modern popular holiday resort began to develop half a mile further on. Its eastern neighbour Sandown was later still in its rise, and has less to offer apart from its long wide strand of golden sands.

Inland across the East Yar is Brading, which once returned two members to Parliament but is now no more than a large village. It has an interesting church with a Transitional nave and Early English chancel and tower, adjoining which is a quaint little old town hall; and at Nunwell nearby the Oglander family have lived since the Norman Conquest, their present house dating from the seventeenth century. But it is for its Roman villa that Brading is most celebrated. Covering nearly 300 square feet, and with the divisions of its principal rooms very clearly marked, it is one of the best relics of a Romano-British family residence in the British Isles.

On either side of the mouth of the Yar are St Helens and Bembridge, both quiet and pleasant places very popular with yachtsmen. St Helens has a large village green, a thirteenth-century tower by the edge of the sea which is all that survives of its church, and one of Palmerston's Spithead forts close to its shore; while on the cliffs a mile or two from Bembridge is a noted school founded in 1919 by J. Howard Whitehouse, who had known Ruskin and was greatly influenced by him. It its grounds are galleries containing the most important collection of Ruskin's drawings in existence, as well as works by artists such as Burne-Jones who were associated with him. There is also an art library with many original Ruskin manuscripts. Near the school is the great Culver Cliff, a natural sanctuary for seabirds, and on Bembridge Down above it an obelisk commemorates the first Earl of Yarborough, who was also the first commodore of the Royal Yacht Squadron. Here one may sit and watch the splendid spectacle of a ceaseless procession of ships entering or leaving Spithead, some of them ships of war coming from Portsmouth or making for it, but the greater number bound for or leaving Southampton Water where this perambulation of Hampshire began.

Index